Business
BENCHMARK

Upper-Intermediate
Vantage

Personal Study Book

Guy Brook-Hart

CAMBRIDGE
UNIVERSITY PRESS

CAMBRIDGE UNIVERSITY PRESS
Cambridge, New York, Melbourne, Madrid, Cape Town, Singapore,
São Paulo, Delhi, Dubai, Tokyo

Cambridge University Press
The Edinburgh Building, Cambridge CB2 8RU, UK

www.cambridge.org
Information on this title: www.cambridge.org/9780521672917

© Cambridge University Press 2006

First published 2006
7th printing 2010

Printed in the United Kingdom at the University Press, Cambridge

A catalogue record for this publication is available from the British Library

ISBN 978-0-521-67291-7 Personal Study Book Upper-Intermediate/Vantage
ISBN 978-0-521-67116-3 Student's Book BEC Vantage Edition
ISBN 978-0-521-67289-4 Student's Book BULATS Edition Upper-Intermediate with CD-ROM
ISBN 978-0-521-67290-0 Teacher's Resource Book Upper-Intermediate/Vantage
ISBN 978-0-521-67292-4 Audio Cassette BEC Vantage Edition
ISBN 978-0-521-67293-1 Audio CD BEC Vantage Edition
ISBN 978-0-521-67659-5 Audio Cassette BULATS Edition Upper-Intermediate
ISBN 978-0-521-67660-1 BULATS Edition Upper-Intermediate Audio CD

Author's note

To the student

This Personal Study Book provides you with two pages of extra exercises and activities for each unit of the Student's Book. The exercises and activities are designed to reinforce what you have studied and they cover vocabulary, grammar, reading and writing.

It is a good idea to do the work in each unit of the Personal Study Book *after* you have finished the unit in the Student's Book. This will help you to remember things you have studied. You will need to write your answers in your notebook. Do the exercises regularly while the things you have studied in the Student's Book are still fresh in your memory.

Check your answers by looking in the key on pages 71–80. If you are not sure why an answer in the key is correct, ask your teacher to explain.

When you do the writing exercises, you can compare your answer with a sample answer in the answer key. If your teacher agrees, you can give him/her your answer to correct.

If you are preparing for the Cambridge ESOL BEC Vantage exam or the BULATS test, many of the exercises are designed to give you exam practice.

The Personal Study Book also contains a Word list. These are words and phrases from the units and recording transcripts of the Student's Book which may be unfamiliar to you, or difficult to understand. When you find new words in the Student's Book, always try to guess the meaning first from the context. Keep a list of new vocabulary in your notebook. In general, use the Word list to check the meanings later, not while you are doing the exercises in the Student's Book.

Acknowledgements

The author and publishers are grateful to the following for permission to reproduce copyright material. It has not always been possible to identify the sources of all the material used. In such cases the publishers would welcome information from the copyright owners.

p.24: Petpals (UK) Limited (http://petpals.com) for the adapted text from 'Why Brendan is Animal Crackers'; p.38: Time Inc. for the article 'What the Web Taught FedEX' by Owen Thomas, from Business 2.0, 18 November 2004, © 2005 Business 2.0 Media Inc.

Illustrations by Tim Oliver (pages 31, 40, and 49)
Design and Layout: Hart McLeod
Project management: Jane Coates
Edited by: Catriona Watson-Brown
Production controller: Gemma Wilkins
Editorial manager: Charlotte Adams
Senior commissioning editor: Sally Searby

Contents

Staff development and training

Vocabulary

1 a Complete the text with the words in the box.

boss
careers
contracts
course
degree
employees
employer
employs
profession
qualifications
~~recruit~~
skills

Our company uses a professional agency to **1** .recruit. new **2** .... The company is a management consultancy, so most new workers have a university **3** .... , even if they have little experience in this particular **4** .... Also, it's quite typical for people to have done other jobs during their **5** .... before becoming management consultants. The company **6** .... about 500 people. For the first two years, workers are on temporary **7** .... , but after that, people are usually made permanent. I think our company is a good **8** .... – new employees are given an induction **9** .... when they start, and on-the-job training to pick up the necessary **10** .... to do our work well, and the professional **11** .... which are expected by our clients. Also, we're closely supervised, and my **12** .... , Adam, regularly appraises my progress both formally and informally.

b Now use the same words to write a paragraph about your company, or a company you know well.

2 Brainstorm words connected with staff training. When you have finished, check for more words by looking at Unit 1 in the Student's Book.

3 Write a brief paragraph describing staff training in the place where you work. See how many of the words from the list in Exercise 1 you can use.

Grammar

1 Look at this leaflet from the Skills Development College and complete the report on the next page by putting the adjectives in brackets into the comparative or superlative form.

SKILLS DEVELOPMENT COLLEGE			
THE SMARTEST WAY TO GET YOUR STAFF UP TO SPEED			
Course	Basic Computer Skills	Advanced Computer Skills	Introduction to Accounting
Length	4 weeks	6 weeks	10 weeks
Hours per week	4	6	8
Timetable	Fri. 4–8 p.m.	Mon. and Weds. 9–12 a.m.	Mon.–Thurs. 8–10 p.m.
Trainees per class	8 max.	6 max.	20 max.
Price (per student)	€200	€300	€150

The Skills Development College offers three courses (see accompanying leaflet) which might meet our staff-training needs during the next year. The one which is **1** l̲e̲a̲s̲t̲ ̲u̲s̲e̲f̲u̲l̲ (useful) is the Basic Computer Skills course, since all our staff have basic computer literacy. The Advanced Computer Skills course could be **2** .... (appropriate), especially for some senior managers who have had little time for intensive training. However, it is scheduled at the **3** .... (inconvenient) time on Monday and Wednesday mornings, just when managers are likely to be **4** .... (busy). In addition, the course is **5** .... (expensive), which means that we will be able to give training to **6** .... (few) staff on our present budget. The course which **7** .... (many) of our junior staff could benefit from is the Introduction to Accounting. This is run outside office hours (8–10 p.m. Mon.–Thurs.), which means that it will have **8** .... (little) effect on the running of our offices. However, it is likely to prove **9** .... (costly) than it appears, as we will have to pay overtime to staff attending the course. Also, the **10** .... (large) size of the classes reflects the fact that the course is **11** .... (theoretical) than the computer-skills courses, which have a **12** .... (hands-on) approach.

2 a Complete the text with a verb from the box in the correct tense – past simple or present perfect.

I **1** ..j̲o̲i̲n̲e̲d̲.. BP as a graduate trainee four years ago – I **2** ....
my degree in Mechanical Engineering at Leeds University – and
they obviously **3** .... right at the beginning that I **4** ....
someone they wanted to keep, so they **5** .... me on the fast
track to promotion. This meant that I **6** .... just three months
in the production department and then they **7** .... me to
marketing. Since then, I **8** .... in three different divisions of
the company and I **9** .... an overseas posting as well – I
10 .... assistant divisional manager in Venezuela for six
months last year. The company **11** .... me to continue
training, and last month I **12** .... my professional exams and
13 .... a member of the Institute of Chartered Engineers.

be
be
become
decide
do
do
do
encourage
~~joined~~
move
put
spend
work

b Write a similar paragraph to describe your own professional career.

Job descriptions and job satisfaction

Vocabulary

1 Circle the odd one out. Check in the Word list if necessary.

1 CEO   PA   CIO   (IT)
2 post   place   job   role
3 local   premises   headquarters   regional office
4 board member   manager   client   director
5 accountant   systems analyst   auditor   financial director
6 white-collar worker   office worker   administrative officer   shop-floor worker
7 secretary   personal assistant   company secretary   administrative assistant
8 advertising   public relations   human resources   marketing

2 a Complete the text with the words in the box.

In my company, nearly all work is done in **1** ....*teams*.... , and all
our managers are **2** .... I found this quite easy to adapt
to, because at Business School, we worked a lot together on
3 .... , and this got me used to working towards goals or
4 .... and meeting **5** .... I work in Research and
Development of new products, and we get real satisfaction from
taking new products through from the original idea to the
6 .... perhaps one or two years later. I'm a financial
manager, so a lot of my work involves ensuring high **7** ....
in our projects while they keep within their **8** .... – and that
involves strict cost control.

budgets
deadlines
launch
performance
projects
targets
team leaders
~~teams~~

**b Use some of the words to write a paragraph about yourself or your
organisation. This will help you to personalise and remember them.**

> Compound nouns (e.g. *human resources manager, team leaders*) are very common
> in business English. Compound nouns have two or more elements. The first
> element is made from a noun (e.g. *team leader*) or a verb (e.g. *working day*).
> The second element is a noun.

**3 How many compound nouns can you make by combining a word from
box A with one from box B? In some cases, more than one combination is
possible.**

A

finance   job
team   product
advertising   office
sales   work

B

budget   development
forecast   manager
satisfaction   work
place   worker

4 Complete the following table.

Verb	Noun	Adjective
1	satisfaction	**2**
develop	**3**	**4**
supervise	**5**	
manage	**6**	**7**
introduce	**8**	**9**
recruit	**10**	
11	**12**	challenging

Grammar

1 Complete these questions with the question words/phrases in the box. You will not need all the words/phrases.

1 .....Who..... is your boss? Ms Jones?
2 .... have you worked for this company?
3 .... office would you prefer to work in: company headquarters or a regional office?
4 .... did you go to school – in this country or abroad?
5 .... does your HR department carry out formal appraisals – every six months, or more often?
6 .... job would you like to be doing in ten years' time?
7 .... people work in your office?
8 .... does your boss earn?

> how
> how long
> how many
> how much
> how often
> what
> when
> where
> which
> ~~who~~
> why

2 Put the words into the correct order to form questions. Write your answers in your notebook.

1 enjoy job do about What your most you?
2 your there about you job anything Is dislike?
3 How discipline you to often workers have do?
4 many are your people there How store in?
5 work of line this into get you did How?
6 What think years' you time you in will be do doing ten?

3 Each of these questions has a mistake. Correct them.

       have you
1 How long ~~you have~~ worked for this company?
2 When you left school?
3 How much are you earn in your present job?
4 If we give you the job, when you can to start?
5 What studied you at university?
6 How long you expect to stay with us?
7 Are you need to speak English in your present job?
8 What you find most challenging in your job?

Letters of enquiry and applications

Grammar

1 Complete this letter of enquiry by putting the correct preposition in each space.

Dear Sir or Madam,

I am a 22-year-old student **1** ...of..... psychology **2** .... the University of Hanover in Germany and I am writing to enquire **3** .... career opportunities **4** .... your company. I have visited your website and I see that you have an innovative and open-minded approach **5** .... the recruitment and management **6** .... personnel within your company. I am **7** .... my final year of a five-year course of studies and am particularly interested **8** .... working **9** .... the area of personnel recruitment. My particular specialisation is psychometric testing, and **10** .... my final project, I have investigated the efficiency of such tests **11** .... predicting the work performance of prospective employees. I would be most grateful if you could send me information **12** .... what opportunities exist in your company, either **13** .... a graduate trainee **14** .... a year s time or for an internship **15** .... the near future. Could you also tell me how I should apply?

Thanking you **16** .... advance.

Yours faithfully,

2 Make these direct questions more formal by starting them with the words given. If necessary, check how to do this by looking at Grammar workshop 1 on page 27 of the Student's Book.

1 When will you be holding interviews?
Could you tell me .when..you..will..be..holding..interviews?..............................

2 How long are the annual holidays?
I would also like to know ....

3 What are the working conditions?
I would be grateful if you could give me information on ....

4 When should I apply?
Please let me know ....

5 Is there a graduate trainee programme?
I would like to know ....

6 Do you offer internships for undergraduates?
Could you tell me ....

Reading

Read the following letter of application. In most lines, there is one extra word. It is either grammatically incorrect or does not fit in with the meaning of the text. Some lines, however, are correct. If a line is correct, put a tick (✓). If there is an extra word in the line, underline it.

Dear Sir,	
I am writing <u>for</u> to apply for the post of manager in your new branch	1 for
to be opened in Lewisham, as advertised in the Daily Gazette of	2 ✓
5 November.	
As you will now see from my enclosed curriculum vitae, I am a	3
33-year-old graduate qualification in social sciences from the	4
University of Bristol, with eight years' of experience in management	5
posts within the retail trade, my current position is being that of	6
assistant manager at a branch of Dixons in Southampton.	7
Since my leaving university, apart from practical experience in the	8
various posts I have held, although I have studied extensively at	9
night school, attending courses in Negotiating Skills, Personnel	10
Management and Marketing. Dixons have also sent for me on	11
various of internal courses in the same areas.	12
I am so interested in the post advertised because it seems to me	13
to represent the type of opportunity I am looking for – to move into a	14
large international retailing organisation and going to have the	15
experience of setting up a new store from the start.	16
I hope for my application and my curriculum vitae will be of	17
interest to you. I am available for interview at any other time, and	18
my present employers would be happy to supply you a reference.	19
I am look forward to hearing from you.	20
Yours faithfully,	

Vocabulary

Match the words (1–6) with their definitions (a–f).

1 challenging   a   difficult, in a way that tests your ability
2 reputation   b   things you get because of your job that are additional to
3 atmosphere   your pay but are not money
4 promotion   c   the character or feeling of a place
5 benefits   d   the opinion that people in general have about someone or
6 scope   something
               e   the opportunity for doing something
               f   when someone is raised to a higher position

4 Telephone skills

Reading

1 Read this advice on speaking on the telephone in English and look at the conversations below and on the opposite page. Find examples of each piece of advice. The advice may be found in one, two or all of the conversations. Write your answers in your notebook.

1 When you answer the telephone at work, give your name or the name of your department. If you are taking an external call, give the name of the company.

A *Christa Schmidt, Marine Division*

B *Logistics*

C *Cranfield Business School*

2 We say *Good afternoon* from about 1 p.m., *Good evening* from about 5.30 and *Good night* when going to bed, or not seeing each other again that night – not generally on the telephone.

3 When speaking to people you know, don't say *I'm Mark Dunhill*.

4 Business people are busy, so give the subject of the call. You can also say *I'm calling in connection with ...*

5 In other words: *Nigel Payne is the person speaking*.

6 You say *My name's ...* only when you are introducing yourself for the first time.

7 Native English speakers say *please* and *thank you* a lot!

8 You can say *Hold on* or *Hang on a minute* if you are speaking informally to someone you know.

9 More polite and formal than saying (in Britain) *Who's that?* and (in the USA) *Who's this?* You can also say *Who is calling, please?*

10 You say this when you connect someone to a different line.

11 Another way of saying this is *Would you like to leave a message?*

A

■ Christa Schmidt, Marine Division. How can I help you?

● Hello. My name's Sandra Dufois. Can I speak to Paola Beluchi, please?

■ I'm afraid she's in a meeting at the moment. Can I take a message?

● Yes. Could you ask her to phone me urgently when she comes out?

■ Certainly. She should be out in about half an hour. I'll get her to give you a ring.

● Thank you. Goodbye.

■ Goodbye.

B
■ Logistics. Can I help you?
● Good afternoon. Can I speak to Nigel Payne, please?
■ Speaking.
● Hello. Mark Dunhill here. I'm just calling to let you know we have received the consignment and that everything is in order.
■ Good. Thank you for calling. Goodbye.
● Goodbye.
C
■ Cranfield Business School. Can I help you?
● Hello. Could I speak to Professor Elgin, please?
■ Yes, can you tell me your name, please, and I'll put you through?
● This is one of his ex-students, Salome Fuster, from Salamanca, Spain.
■ Hold on a moment, please. I'll put you through.
● Thank you.

2 Complete these telephone conversations by putting one word in each space.

MARIBEL: Finance department. **1** .... can I help you?
MANFRED: Good morning. Can I speak **2** .... Maribel Arroyo, please?
MARIBEL: **3** ....
MANFRED: Oh, hello. **4** .... is Manfred Steiner from Arts International.
MARIBEL: Hello, Mr Steiner. What can I do **5** .... you?
MANFRED: Well, it's about an invoice – you sent the order we placed, but you forgot to include the invoice, so we can't pay you.
MARIBEL: Oh, that's not my department, I'm **6** .... , Mr Steiner. That's Mary Slade in Invoicing.
MANFRED: OK. Can I speak to her then, please?
MARIBEL: Sure. I'll put you **7** ....
MANFRED: Thanks very much.
MARIBEL: Not at **8** ....

JANE: Jane Ashley.
ALAN: Oh, hello, Jane, I've been trying to call Tracy, but she's not answering the phone, and it's rather urgent.
JANE: Who is **9** .... , please?
ALAN: **10** .... is Alan Searle.
JANE: Oh, hello, Alan, I didn't recognise your voice. I'm **11** .... she's in a meeting at the moment and she's left instructions that she's not to be disturbed. Can I **12** .... a message?
ALAN: Yes, can you ask her to call me as soon as **13** .... ?
JANE: Yes, of **14** ....
ALAN: **15** .... you very much. Bye.
JANE: Goodbye.

UNIT 5 Promotional activities and branding

Vocabulary

Read this text about inventors and choose the best word, A, B, C or D, to fill each gap.

It is not easy for inventors to **1** ..B.... a new product on the market, especially when they have to **2** .... with large consumer products companies which have a marketing **3** .... of millions of pounds. Essentially, inventors have to carry out market **4** .... beforehand in order to discover who might need or want their product, and what **5** .... they might be prepared to pay. For a small company, the most effective marketing **6** .... is to demonstrate the product to potential customers first, so that they know what they are buying. **7** .... your marketing efforts on the customers you have and make sure to keep them happy and **8** .... If you can do that, you will discover that they talk about the product to other people, and **9** .... recommendation is the most cost-effective way of extending your customer base.

Before undertaking costly **10** .... activities, such as printing brochures and taking out advertisements, use your imagination to see if you can reach your **11** .... customers without spending so much. Relatively cheap ways of marketing your product are through a(n) **12** .... , handing out free **13** .... at big events, and sending your product to journalists, who, if the product interests them, may write an article about it in a magazine or newspaper. All these activities will raise brand **14** ....

Be ready to sell directly to customers, but, if your product is a consumer product, it is worth approaching retail stores to see if they will **15** .... it, too.

1 **A** introduce	**B** launch	**C** establish	**D** start
2 **A** compete	**B** fight	**C** oppose	**D** struggle
3 **A** resource	**B** fund	**C** budget	**D** account
4 **A** research	**B** investigation	**C** experiments	**D** study
5 **A** money	**B** number	**C** total	**D** price
6 **A** manoeuvre	**B** scheme	**C** move	**D** ploy
7 **A** Employ	**B** Focus	**C** Aim	**D** Direct
8 **A** constant	**B** true	**C** loyal	**D** faithful
9 **A** word-of-mouth	**B** mouth-to-mouth	**C** face-to-face	**D** eye-to-eye
10 **A** publicity	**B** promotional	**C** selling	**D** sales
11 **A** end	**B** aim	**C** target	**D** object
12 **A** Internet	**B** email	**C** hyperlink	**D** website
13 **A** examples	**B** copies	**C** samples	**D** trials
14 **A** understanding	**B** awareness	**C** knowledge	**D** information
15 **A** hold	**B** have	**C** keep	**D** stock

Grammar

1 Complete the following job advertisement with *a/an* if the noun is countable and singular. Leave the space blank if the noun is uncountable or plural.

Looking for **1** .... work in **2** .... advertising? Blatch and Moore is recruiting **3** .... writer to prepare the copy for **4** .... direct mailshots. You may also from time to time be asked to write **5** .... advertisement or leaflet. **6** .... formal qualifications are not necessary, but **7** .... experience in **8** .... marketing is desirable. We are offering **9** .... permanent contract to the right person. **10** .... satisfactory performance will lead to **11** .... quick promotion. For the right person, our company is **12** .... business with **13** .... future!

2 Complete this email from the CEO of a company to the finance director by putting the verbs in brackets into the correct form: *-ing* form or infinitive. (For when to use *-ing* forms and infinitives, look at Grammar workshop 2 on page 45 in the Student's Book.)

Dear Colin,

I am writing **1** to express (express) my concern about the situation of several of our product lines. Sales appear **2** .... (be) falling in several of them. I suggest **3** .... (increase) our marketing budget this year by about 20%. I think we will have **4** .... (spend) more on advertising in order **5** .... (raise) brand awareness. Competition in our sector has been increasing, and we have to avoid **6** .... (lose) market share to our competitors, which is something we risk **7** .... (do) by **8** .... (follow) our present strategy. Also, by **9** .... (contact) our main customers directly, we may be able **10** .... (find) out why our products are losing competitiveness. I think it would be worth **11** .... (do) this, and also **12** .... (think) about **13** .... (develop) new lines and **14** .... (innovate) a bit more. Perhaps we could arrange **15** .... (meet) sometime **16** .... (discuss) this. I would be happy **17** .... (see) you any time next week.
Looking forward to **18** .... (hear) from you,

Vince

New product development

Vocabulary

1 Complete the table by writing nouns, verbs and adjectives in the numbered spaces.

Verb	Noun	Adjective
1	founder	
	entrepreneur	**2**
	skill	**3**
commute	**4**	
launch	**5**	
establish	**6**	**7**
opt	**8**	**9**
rely	**10**	**11**

2 Choose the correct answer, A, B or C.

1 What is the marketing term for a sales representative who visits customers to sell a product?
   A visiting   **B** direct selling   **C** travelling

2 A luxury product which is high quality and expensive is a(n) .... product.
   A upmarket   **B** downmarket   **C** middle-market

3 A product which only appeals to a very specialist group of customers is a .... product.
   A special   **B** niche   **C** reserved

4 The percentage of the market which your company has is your market ....
   A quota   **B** segment   **C** share

5 What is a brand called which has the supermarket's name on it?
   A an own brand   **B** a white brand   **C** a proprietary brand

6 Which word has these three meanings: *start (a company), put (a product) on the market, start (an advertising campaign)?*
   A throw   **B** begin   **C** launch

7 What do marketers call the place where the product reaches the consumer?
   A an end-user   **B** a final stop   **C** an outlet

8 What is another word for direct mail?
   A correspondence   **B** junk mail   **C** snail mail

9 When a company subsidises a football team or a music concert, what is this called?
   A endorsement   **B** subvention   **C** sponsorship

10 Which of these publicity materials is likely to look like a colour magazine?
   A a brochure   **B** a leaflet   **C** a newsletter
11 When a company does a lot of publicity, this is called ....
   A an advertising campaign   **B** a promotional event   **C** a price war
12 When clients or consumers talk about your product or service, what is this
   type of publicity called?
   A a talking campaign   **B** word-of-mouth   **C** personal
                                                         recommendations

Grammar

1 Janice and Martin opened a chocolate shop in their town. Match the first
half of the sentences in column A with the second halves in column B to
complete the explanations of their promotional activities.

A	B
1 We had special offers during the first two weeks	a local people could see where we were and what we were selling.
2 We invited a lot of people to the opening and gave them free samples to get them	b remind people when the shop was opening.
3 We put a front-page ad in the evening newspaper in order to	c talking about the shop to their friends.
4 We sent free samples to local journalists so	d to attract people to visit the shop.
5 We sent leaflets to every house in town so that	e they could write about our products.

2 Read the following paragraph which recommends how a new restaurant
should be promoted. Write one word in each space to complete the
paragraph.

The restaurant should have a website, **1** .... that potential customers
can see the menu and the installations before they come here. **2** ....
would also be a good idea to advertise in local and regional newspapers in
3 .... to make our name known to people in the area. We should also
invite some journalists to eat here, **4** .... that if they like the restaurant,
they can write articles about it. Finally, it's important to give really excellent
food and service **5** .... get people talking about the restaurant,
6 .... word-of-mouth publicity is by far the cheapest and most
effective.

3 You have been asked to write a report recommending ways of promoting
a new hotel in your town or city which is aimed at business travellers.
Write the final paragraph of the report (like the one above), where you
recommend how the hotel can be promoted and you state the purpose
of each promotional method that you recommend.

A stand at a trade fair

Vocabulary

1 **How many compound nouns can you make by combining a word from box A with a word from box B?**

A	food customer event exhibition export floor publicity

B	base centre exhibition markets material organisers space stand

2 **Complete these sentences with a compound noun from Exercise 1.**

1 Can you contact the .... to find out how much it would cost to exhibit?
2 How long does it take to get from the airport to the .... ?
3 I'd prefer to hire an .... rather than custom-build one because we don't have room to store it when it's not in use.
4 It's a good opportunity to meet foreign buyers and have a chance to open new ....
5 We shall need about 40 square metres of .... for our stand.
6 We try to expand our .... by exhibiting at trade fairs.
7 We will need quite a lot of shelves for all our .... such as leaflets, catalogues and brochures.
8 We're hoping to have a stand at the International .... next year.

Writing

1 **Complete this email by writing one word in each space.**

⊖ ⊙ ⊖	In	⊂⊃

Dear Sir/Madam

1 .... are a medium-sized business based in Southampton, England, specialising **2** .... the development and production of marine electronic instruments. We are interested in the possibility **3** .... marketing our products in your country and are contacting companies in the sector **4** .... might be willing to act as agents or distributors for **5** .... products. We wonder **6** .... you would be interested in acting in this role for us. I **7** .... be visiting your country during the first fortnight of next month and would welcome the chance of a meeting with you. **8** .... you suggest a day and a time **9** .... would be convenient for you?I look **10** .... to hearing from you.

Scott Cunliffe
Export Sales Director

---

2 Your boss has asked you to write a reply to the email above. Write the email:
- saying that you would be interested in acting as agents
- saying that your boss would like a meeting
- suggesting a day and a time.

Write 40–50 words.

Reading

There is one extra word in every numbered line of this fax. Underline the extra words.

FAX

Attention: P. Maguire
Managing Director
Electronic Solutions

Dear Miss Maguire

I am delighted to hear that you are interested in being acting as our agent in | 1
New Zealand and I look forward very much to my meeting you at 10.30 on | 2
Monday 7 October. It would also give me a great pleasure to invite you and | 3
the marketing director to lunch after the meeting if you are then free. Do let | 4
me know if this is possible, and, if is so, can I ask you to book a table at | 5
your favourite restaurant?

For your interest, I am not attaching details and technical specifications of | 6
some of our main products on the following pages, also together with a | 7
price list. I am sending to you a complete catalogue by post. | 8

Yours sincerely,

Scott Cunliffe
Export Sales Director

Grammar

Complete these questions, using up to four words in each space.

1 I shall be visiting your city next month. Can you suggest a day when
.... convenient to meet you?

2 We are interested in having a stand at the exhibition. Can ....
space is still available?

3 I have seen your products advertised in various trade journals and I would
like to know .... exhibiting at the coming trade exhibition.

4 I hear that the trade fair will be held in Birmingham this year. Could you
.... days it will be held so that I can keep them free?

5 I am interested in buying the machine you mentioned in your email. Can you
please let me know .... costs?

Establishing relationships and negotiating

Vocabulary

1 Choose the correct way of saying these figures.

1 535
  A five hundred thirty-five
  B five hundred and thirty-five
2 233,499
  A two hundred, thirty-three thousand, four hundred, ninety-nine
  B two hundred and thirty-three thousand, four hundred and ninety-nine
3 2.5
  A two point five
  B two and five
4 10.25
  A ten point twenty-five
  B ten point two five
5 50%
  A a fifty per cent
  B fifty per cent
6 £3.50
  A three pounds fifty
  B three fifty pounds
7 €19.99
  A nineteen euros ninety-nine
  B nineteen euros and ninety-nine
8 €45,000 p.a.
  A forty-five thousand euros a year
  B forty and five thousand euros per year

2 Complete the paragraph below with words from the box. If necessary, check the meanings in the Word list.

We are a small agricultural business which produces oranges for the export market. Our **1** .... , or routine costs, such as water for irrigation or pesticides are pretty high. This means that when we sell our products, our **2** .... is very narrow. Also, we face a lot of competition, so when buyers place **3** .... , they often expect a hefty **4** .... or **5** .... in price. Some years, there's no profit at all. On the other hand, when you go to the supermarket, you see that the same fruit has been given an enormous **6** .... – sometimes as much as 400% – and the **7** .... bears no relation to the price we were given when we sold the oranges.

> bulk orders
> discount
> mark-up
> overheads
> profit margin
> recommended
> retail price
> reductions

Grammar

Put the verbs in brackets into the correct tenses to form first conditional sentences.

1 I 'll give........ (give) you a 15% discount on condition that you pay within 30 days.
2 We .... (not be) able to stay in business unless he .... (pay) in cash.
3 We .... (place) an order for 50,000 units, providing you can get them to us in time for the Christmas season.
4 As long as you .... (guarantee) that we are your sole supplier, we .... (allow) you to have the goods at a special price
5 Unless you pay the full price, we .... (not manage) to cover our overheads.

Reading

Read the following letter. There is an extra word in every numbered line. Underline the extra words.

Dear Mr Markham,	
Late payment	
I regret to say that we have not yet received some payment for the goods that we	1
delivered to you in March, although the agreement was that you would to pay in	2
30 days. This is causing us severe cashflow problems, and unless you will pay us	3
immediately, we will have to stop supplying to you with the goods you require.	4
However, I would also like to warn you that if you do not pay promptly, we will	5
be unable to offer you back your usual discounts in the future.	6
I look forward to be receiving your payment shortly.	7
Yours sincerely,	
Georgina Chandler	
Accounts manager	

Writing

You received the above letter this morning. Write an email to your assistant telling him to:
• investigate the cause of the problem
• pay the invoice
• apologise and explain to Ms Chandler.

You should write about 40–50 words.

Going it alone

Vocabulary

1 Match the words (1–8) with their definitions (a–h).

1 make a go of
2 running
3 entrepreneur
4 outlet
5 fee
6 redundancy money
7 mortgage
8 retailing

a be successful at
b loan to buy a house
c managing
d money you get from the company when you lose your job
e money you pay for a service
f selling through a shop
g shop or other place where the product reaches the customer
h someone who starts a business

2 Complete the crossword.

Across

1 Total sales minus costs (7)
5 Selling through a shop (9)
6 The place where your business operates from (8)
8 The opposite of assets (11)
10 Someone who starts their own business (12)
11 Finding the money to pay for your business plans (9)
12 Money you get when you lose your job (10, 5)

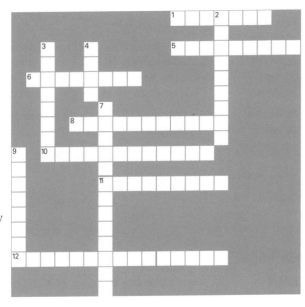

Down

2 A business you operate under licence from a larger company (9)
3 A loan from a bank to buy a house (8)
4 Go bankrupt (4)
7 A prediction of how much a company will sell (5, 8)
9 Total sales (8)

3 a Look at the words in the box and say which word refers to …

1 the organisation which gives franchises
2 the person or company which receives a franchise licence.

franchisee
franchiser

b Make similar words from these verbs.

1 employ   2 interview   3 train   4 pay

4 Complete these sentences with the words in the box.

1 Another word for total sales is ....
2 Factories and other property are fixed ....
3 Our debts are ....
4 Our pre-tax .... are up by 25% this year.
5 Salaries have risen, which means that staff .... are higher.
6 The interest .... is 6.5%.
7 We have to pay a .... on profits of 25%.

assets
costs
liabilities
profits
rate
tax
turnover

5 Put the correct form of *do*, *make* or *go* in each space.

My dream is to **1** ...make... as much money as possible as quickly as possible, and I believe that the only way to **2** .... this is to speculate. Basically, speculating is **3** .... investments when things are cheap, then hoping they will **4** .... up in price very quickly, then selling. It's not the same as **5** .... a job, of course, and you need some capital to start with. Also, there's the risk that you will lose your investment and **6** .... bankrupt. On the other hand, if you have the money, it's easier than **7** .... into business, but perhaps less satisfying.

Grammar

Put the verbs in brackets into the correct tense.

1 When I ...was... (*be*) at university, I studied Business Administration and Accountancy.
2 I suddenly had an idea for a business start-up while I .... (*study*) at university.
3 In ten years' time, when my business .... (*be*) established, I hope I will be able to relax more.
4 I hope sales will improve when the Christmas season .... (*start*).
5 He hopes to work in a consultancy after he .... (*leave*) university.
6 The meeting started before all the sales staff .... (*arrive*).
7 Send that letter by courier as soon as you .... (*write*) it.
8 Tell her to come to my office as soon as she .... (*arrive*).
9 You'll never know if your business idea will be a success until you .... (*try*).
10 He knew he had made a mistake as soon as he .... (*send*) the email.

10 Financing the start-up

Vocabulary

Read this story about someone who joined a franchise called Petpals, which looks after people's domestic animals while they are working or on holiday. Choose the best answer, A, B, C or D, to fill each space.

Brendan Humphrey of Petpals Winchester says, 'I **1** .... my £40,000-a-year job as a surveyor to join the franchise, **2** .... up all the associated stress, and have not missed a single moment of the old job. It was hard work for the first year, as I was **3** .... my business and we had to be careful with money, but what a great year! I could not believe it; in our first year, our turnover **4** .... just over £35,000, producing around £10,000 **5** .... profit, and we even managed to **6** .... most of our finance. No more stresses and strains of the old life, I have lost weight, have peace of mind, sanity and probably the best job in the world.' Petpals Winchester now **7** .... four part-time assistants and is growing at a controlled **8** .... of around 20% a quarter. Part of a famous rock band that started back in the sixties, Richard Herd, of Petpals Saffron Walden wanted a business that he could **9** .... with his wife, Pauline. That would allow them to work together in harmony while **10** .... a rewarding service to busy pet owners. Richard and Pauline say, 'We enjoy being very much part of the franchise. Support is always on **11** .... if we need it.'

1	**A** stopped	**B** threw	**C** went	**D** quit
2	**A** leaving	**B** giving	**C** throwing	**D** stopping
3	**A** growing	**B** doing	**C** looking	**D** working
4	**A** arrived	**B** reached	**C** rose	**D** met
5	**A** complete	**B** large	**C** gross	**D** top
6	**A** pay up	**B** pay in	**C** pay out	**D** pay off
7	**A** employs	**B** contracts	**C** engages	**D** hires
8	**A** amount	**B** percentage	**C** number	**D** rate
9	**A** work	**B** run	**C** do	**D** make
10	**A** sending	**B** paying	**C** providing	**D** renting
11	**A** hand	**B** paper	**C** reach	**D** side

Grammar

1 Put the verbs in brackets into the correct tenses to form second conditionals.

1 If interest rates ..weren't... (*not be*) so high, I would take out. (*take out*) a loan from the bank.

2 Banks .... (*not lend*) you money unless they .... (*be*) sure you could pay it back.

3 If offices .... (*be*) cheaper, I ....(*start*) my business in the
   centre of London.
4 If it .... (*not be*) such hard work, I .... (*open*) a restaurant.
5 He knew he .... (*never get*) rich unless he .... (*start*) his own
   business.
6 If my overheads .... (*be*) lower, my profits .... (*be*) higher.

**2 Change these pieces of advice to sentences beginning with *If I were
    you* ...**

1 You should work harder.
   If I were you, I'd work harder. ....

2 You should do some market research before starting up.
   ....

3 Why don't you see if your family will lend you the money?
   ....

4 You ought to lease the equipment you need instead of buying it.
   ....

5 I think you should buy the premises, not rent them.
   ....

6 It would be a good idea to do the accounts yourself. That way you'll save
   money.

Writing

1 Complete the following letter by putting one word in each space.

Dear Mr Allen,

Thank you **1** .... your letter of 14 June in **2** .... you apply for
a Young Entrepreneur's Grant to help you set **3** .... your business.

We would be very happy **4** .... consider your application and in any case
offer **5** .... advice which you may find useful. We would like to invite
you to **6** .... interview where we can discuss your application
7 .... Monday 1 July.

Please telephone me to **8** .... me know if the date is convenient, or if
9 .... , to arrange a different **10** ....

Yours sincerely,

Gudrun Lear

**2 Your boss has received a letter from a student called Mary Hall, who
    would like to gain work experience with your company. He has asked you
    to write a letter in reply in which you should:**

• invite the person for an interview
• say when and where the interview will be held
• ask the person to phone you to confirm the time.

Use the letter above as a model.

Vocabulary

1 Circle the odd word out in each set.

1 secretary   PA   (CEO)   typist
2 headquarters   head office   branch   HQ
3 warehouse   stockroom   showroom   storeroom
4 shop floor   boardroom   factory   production facility
5 facility   shop   outlet   store
6 the board   shareholders   management   directors
7 back office   research facility   laboratory   R&D
8 develop   innovate   modify   launch

2 a Combine words in box A with words in box B to make compound nouns or adjectives.

A	cold cost eye ground job knowledge problem record team time

B	breaking building calling catching consuming cutting sharing solving

b Use the compound nouns to complete these sentences.

1 A lot of you haven't worked together before, so before we start on the project, we're going to do some .... activities together.

2 He only wants to work part-time, so he's interested in a .... arrangement with someone else in the office.

3 I find a lot of this paperwork very .... , which is frustrating and stops me getting on with more vital work.

4 In our laboratories in South Africa, we're doing some .... , totally innovative research.

5 The main purpose of this meeting is .... , so that at the end of the meeting, we'll all have told each other what we know about the latest marketing techniques.

6 Phoning a potential client whom you have never spoken to before – .... – is the part of my job I like least.

7 The company is doing some .... by relocating headquarters out of the centre of town to a cheaper area.

8 The purpose of this brainstorming session is to think of some .... ideas to get us out of our present difficulties.

9 The shareholders are really happy this year because our company has made .... profits.

10 We need .... displays of our best products in our showroom.

Reading

Read this proposal. There is one wrong word in every line. Cross out the wrong word and write the correct word.

Proposal for launching our products in Eastern Europe

Introduction

The purpose ~~for~~ this proposal is to suggest that we market our products | 1 *of*
in Eastern Europe and to present a plot of action. | 2

Current situation

In present, our main markets are Western Europe, North America and | 3
Japan. Although, as many countries in Eastern Europe have recently | 4
joined the EU, there is a new market close from our production facilities | 5
what is becoming more prosperous. | 6

Market research

Initially, it should be a good idea to carry out market research to find | 7
out:
• who our competitors will become in the market | 8
• which prices customers would be prepared to pay | 9
• which retail shops would be suitable and willing to sell our products. | 10

Finding an agent or distributor

I suggested we place an advertisement in a trade journal in each of | 11
the target countries, inviting potential agents or distributors to fix | 12
contact with us. Members of the marketing band should then visit | 13
the countries and meet the agents in time to assess which would be | 14
the more suitable and to negotiate a business arrangement. | 15

Conclusion

I recommend that we should start investigating this markets | 16
straightaway and aim to put our products in those countries in | 17
between six months to the year. The finance department should | 18
set aside a budget of £50,000 in this activity. | 19

Grammar

Join these sentences using the words given. Write your answers in your notebook.

1 He's very competent. He never got promotion. (*despite*)
   Despite being very competent, he never got promotion.
2 They had a large budget. They ran short of money. (*although*)
3 We carried out market research. Our product failed. (*in spite of*)
4 The company was extremely successful. It had cashflow problems. (*although*)
5 We decided to rent the premises. The premises were extremely expensive. (*despite*)
6 Our agent didn't understand the market. He was a local man. (*although*)
7 We spent over £1m on advertising. Brand awareness didn't improve. (*in spite of*)

12 Presenting your business idea

Vocabulary

1 Match the pieces of equipment in the box to their descriptions.

1 These are often photocopies. You can include complex information which is difficult to explain and hand them out to people.

2 This is a computer you can carry around, so it's great for taking to a presentation.

3 This is where you can project your charts and slides so that everyone in the room can see them.

4 You can hand these round so people can actually handle and see what you are talking about.

5 You can operate equipment from anywhere in the room using this.

6 You can use this to point at things on the screen, and a little red light will shine where you point it.

7 You can use this to show information from a computer on a large screen.

8 You can write notes on these large pages before your lecture and just turn them over when you need them. Also, you can write here during your talk.

> data projector
> flipchart
> handouts
> laptop
> pointer
> remote control
> product samples
> screen

2 Match the sentence beginnings (1–9) with the sentence endings (a–i) to make typical signalling phrases for presentations.

1 Good afternoon and

2 Thank you for

3 Let me introduce myself:

4 What I would like to do in this presentation is

5 My presentation will have four parts.

6 If you have any questions while I'm speaking,

7 Now, I'd like to conclude by

8 Finally, let me finish by saying

9 Now if you have any other questions, I'd

a describe this company to you and outline our business plans for the next year.

b don't hesitate to interrupt me.

c finding the time to come today.

d be happy to answer them.

e my name's Fatima Belenguer.

f summarising my main points again.

g that it's been a pleasure talking to you, and thank you for your time.

h The first part will be to tell you what our company does.

i welcome to the offices of Quickinvest Ltd.

Grammar

1 Read this extract from a presentation and put the verbs in brackets into the correct form.

Good morning, and welcome to the Strand Hotel. Thank you all very much for
1 .... (*come*); some of you **2** .... (*travel*) a long way
3 .... (*hear*) us today, and I hope you **4** .... (*all have*) good
journeys. So let me **5** .... (*introduce*) myself: my name's Peter Furlong,
and this is my partner, Mark Davies.

The purpose of this presentation is **6** .... (*explain*) our business plans
to you and hopefully to get you interested in **7** .... (*invest*) in our new
company, Clock Options Express.

In my presentation, I **8** .... (*hope*) to do three things. First, I
9 .... (*give*) you a short summary of our main business idea. Then I
10 .... (*tell*) you the findings of the market research that we
11 .... (*conduct*), and finally I **12** .... (*outline*) our financial
requirements and plans, which should show you what a sound and exciting
investment Clock Options Express **13** .... (*represent*). If you have any
questions you **14** .... (*like*) to ask, please leave them to the end when I
15 .... (*be*) very happy **16** .... (*answer*) them.

2 Choose the best modal verb, A, B or C, for each gap.

1 I think we ...... raise production levels to meet growing demand – it's not
absolutely necessary because we still have stocks, but it would be a good idea.
A must   **B** may   **C** should

2 I don't know what our competitors are going to do. They ...... possibly lower
their prices, I suppose, although that will have an effect on their profit
margins.
A must   **B** may   **C** should

3 You ...... come into the office early tomorrow – it's essential we discuss things
before the meeting.
A must   **B** may   **C** could

4 Be careful of Bill Watson. He ...... get very irritable if you interrupt him when
he's busy.
A must   **B** can   **C** should

5 I'm sorry. It's been useful talking to you, but I ...... go now. I have a client
waiting for me outside.
A might   **B** can   **C** have to

6 If you have difficulty concentrating in the office, you ...... take the work home
to complete there – I don't mind.
A can   **B** might   **C** have to

7 I was thinking that in the future I ...... start my own business – that is, if I can
save enough money from this job first.
A can   **B** have to   **C** might

8 Now that you've completed the training course, I'm sure you ...... deal with
customers without me supervising you.
A must   **B** might   **C** can

UNIT 13 Business hotels and sales conferences

Vocabulary

1 Complete this letter by choosing the most appropriate word, A, B, C or D, for each gap.

Dear Sirs,

Please **1** ...... a single room **2** ...... bath for me for the nights **3** ...... 18 and 19 March. If possible, I would like the room to **4** ...... in a quiet part of the hotel.

I shall **5** ...... to meet a **6** ...... of clients on the morning of 20 March, **7** ...... could you make a meeting room available **8** ...... me on that day from 9 a.m. to 2 p.m.?

I do not expect to arrive until about 11 p.m. on 18 March, so please **9** ...... my room for me. Also, please fax me as soon as possible to **10** ...... that these bookings have been made. If you **11** ...... me to send a deposit in **12** ...... , let me know and I shall be happy to do so.

Yours faithfully,

---

1 **A** hold	**B** reserve	**C** get	**D** give
2 **A** with	**B** consisting	**C** including	**D** containing
3 **A** on	**B** of	**C** for	**D** in
4 **A** situate	**B** locate	**C** be	**D** place
5 **A** like	**B** prefer	**C** need	**D** think
6 **A** quantity	**B** number	**C** selection	**D** range
7 **A** for	**B** then	**C** so	**D** consequently
8 **A** for	**B** from	**C** with	**D** of
9 **A** have	**B** reserve	**C** maintain	**D** keep
10 **A** ensure	**B** promise	**C** confirm	**D** agree
11 **A** demand	**B** require	**C** hope	**D** oblige
12 **A** ahead	**B** advance	**C** preparation	**D** priority

2 Look at the bar chart at the top of the next page and complete this paragraph using the words from the box.

In our **1** .... of 600 business travellers, we **2** .... that 42% considered preferential service was the most important **3** .... , whereas 35% **4** .... good food and drink as the most important, and 23% valued comfortable seats most **5** ....

amenity
found
highly
rated
survey

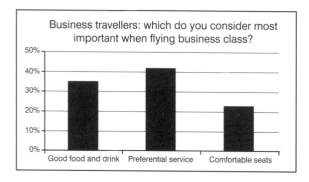

3 Write a paragraph describing this pie chart.

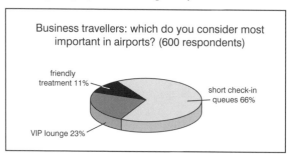

Grammar

1 Complete the sentences below by putting the verbs in brackets into the correct forms.

1 The plane was delayed and they didn't tell us. They .should have told. (*should/tell*) us as soon as they knew.

2 I thought the aircraft was pretty dirty. They .... (*should/clean*) it properly before we got on board.

3 They allowed the economy-class passengers to board first. I think they .... (*should/allow*) the business-class passengers to go first.

4 The steward gave me the same food as the economy-class passengers. I think he .... (*should/give*) me better food.

5 We had to queue to get off the plane. We .... (*should/not/have*) to queue.

2 Complete these sentences in any way you like using the form *should have* + past participle.

1 There was nobody waiting for me at the airport. They ....

2 The bank was closed when I arrived, so I couldn't change money. The bank ....

3 The customs officer was rude when he searched my luggage. He ....

4 It took over an hour for my luggage to come through to the baggage reclaim. They ....

14 Business conferences

Vocabulary

1 Choose the correct word, A, B, C or D, to complete each of these sentences.

1 Phil Davies works for a ......-making organisation whose aim is to encourage local people to start their own business.
   A no profit   **B** non-profit   **C** no benefit   **D** unprofitable

2 There are great opportunities for our company in ...... markets where products like ours haven't been sold before.
   A opening   **B** appearing   **C** emerging   **D** arising

3 You should study the market ...... if you want to know how the market is going to behave in the future.
   A indicators   **B** signs   **C** signals   **D** indications

4 One of the best ways of ...... company image is to provide first-class customer service.
   A enhancing   **B** bettering   **C** growing   **D** increasing

5 This course will provide trainees with ...... experience of business travel-booking procedures.
   A touching   **B** contact   **C** hands-on   **D** fingertip

6 After the board has given its approval, it will be my job to supervise the ...... of the new marketing plan.
   A practising   **B** improvisation **C** realisation   **D** implementation

7 During the conference, there will be numerous opportunities for ...... , when delegates will be able to talk to each other about their experiences and interests.
   A brainstorming **B** hot desking   **C** teleworking   **D** networking

8 Dr Soames' talk provided delegates with some valuable ...... into the role of dotcom companies in emerging markets.
   A views   **B** insights   **C** explanations **D** understanding

9 Dr Sloane is a(n) ...... speaker, and we're very fortunate to have him here to deliver the keynote speech this morning.
   A distinct   **B** outstanding   **C** striking   **D** extreme

2 Write the opposites of these adjectives.

1 usual   ...unusual........
2 persuasive   ....
3 proven   ....
4 motivating   ....
5 reliable   ....
6 organised   ....
7 communicative   ....

3 Complete the table. In many cases, more than one word is possible. Think of as many as you can.

Noun	Verb	Adjective
persuasion/persuasiveness	persuade	persuasive
1	implement	
2	consult	3
4	exhibit	
5	present	
6	operate	7
8	prove	9
10	combine	11
12	finance	13
14	motivate	15
16	rely	17
18	organise	19
20	communicate	21

4 Complete these sentences with the adjectives from Exercise 3 (either positive or negative).

1 He was an extremely .... speaker, and we all found ourselves agreeing with him.

2 Sheila is so .... that you never know if she will do the job properly or not.

3 I find that, for a salesman, Brian is surprisingly .... and he never really tells you if there are problems or not. You have to find them out for yourself.

4 The conference could have been better .... A lot of the sessions started in chaos.

5 He's an excellent speaker with a .... track record.

6 It's very .... after all the preparation to find that only seven people came to my talk.

5 Complete this description of a conference speaker by putting one word in each space.

Catherine DeVrye (MSc, CSP), is **1** .....the...... best-selling author of *Good Service is Good Business* and winner of the Australian Executive Woman of the Year Award. Catherine is an outstanding communicator, **2** .... proven international management experience **3** .... the private and public sectors. A former IBM executive, Catherine has held roles in sales and marketing, communications and management development. And Catherine **4** .... had practical, hands-on experience in the tourism industry. The title of **5** .... talk today is 'Making Your Destination Attractive' in **6** .... she will **7** .... close attention to the belief **8** .... good service is good business.

Writing

Imagine you are going to give a talk at a conference. Write a similar description of yourself and the talk you are going to give.

Reports

Vocabulary

1 For each gap, choose the best word, A, B, C or D.

Report on the performance of Burford Sports Centre

Introduction

The 1 .... of this report is to show the performance of the Burford Sports Centre last year and its projected performance in the 2 .... year.

Use of Sports Centre

The 3 .... of days that the sports centre is used has 4 .... by approximately 15% this year, from 310 to 362, 5 .... to the fact that it now opens on Sundays. This situation is projected to continue next year as well.

6 .... , the number of members using the sports centre each day has fallen: last year, there was a(n) 7 .... of 163 people per day, whereas the average was just 148 this year. However, this figure is 8 .... to recover next year to approximately 160.

Financial performance

Turnover rose from just 9 .... £5m last year to £5.5m this year, and this positive 10 .... is expected to continue next year. Profits also rose 11 .... this year. They increased by approximately £150,000 from £540,000 to £690,000. Moreover, 12 .... figure is forecasted to rise even 13 .... , to about £800,000 next year.

Conclusion

Our level of activity is 14 .... , and our financial performance is extremely healthy. In the coming year, we may consider reinvesting some of the profits 15 .... renovating the installations.

---

1 **A** motive	**B** reason	**C** purpose	**D** thinking
2 **A** coming	**B** subsequent	**C** following	**D** next
3 **A** figure	**B** number	**C** sum	**D** total
4 **A** risen	**B** raised	**C** boosted	**D** put up
5 **A** due	**B** because	**C** consequence	**D** explained
6 **A** Although	**B** Whereas	**C** While	**D** However
7 **A** figure	**B** number	**C** quantity	**D** average
8 **A** forecast	**B** hoped	**C** planned	**D** thought
9 **A** under	**B** underneath	**C** less	**D** fewer
10 **A** tendency	**B** fashion	**C** trend	**D** direction
11 **A** meaningfully	**B** significantly	**C** emphatically	**D** especially
12 **A** a	**B** the	**C** this	**D** these
13 **A** greater	**B** longer	**C** further	**D** larger
14 **A** enhancing	**B** increasing	**C** accelerating	**D** overtaking
15 **A** in	**B** for	**C** with	**D** to

2 Write 'I' or 'D' for each of these words, according to whether they express increases or decreases.

1 cut	4 go down	7 raise	10 rise
2 drop	5 go up	8 recover	11 soar
3 fall	6 plummet	9 reduce	

3 Study the chart and complete the description using words from Exercise 2.

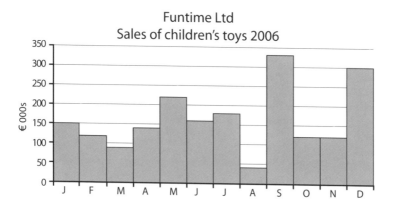

Funtime Ltd
Sales of children's toys 2006

Sales of children's toys **1** .... from £150,000 in January to £90,000 in March. Then they **2** .... to reach £220,000 in May before **3** .... again to £160,000 in June. In July, they **4** .... slightly to £170,000 before **5** .... to £40,000 in August. In September, sales **6** .... to £330,000 and then **7** .... to £120,000 for October and November. In December, they **8** .... once again to £300,000.

Grammar

Put the verbs in brackets into the correct form of the passive.

Nonstop Watches **1** was started (*start*) in 1968 by Ian Murray from a small workshop in his garden in Dundee. Its first product, a waterproof stopwatch, **2** .... (*launch*) the same year and was an immediate success when it **3** .... (*adopt*) as the official stopwatch for the 1968 Highland Games. In 1969, the company moved to a factory just outside Dundee, and in that factory, more than five million watches **4** .... (*produce*) until now. In a constant bid for innovation, the latest digital technology **5** .... (*recently introduce*) to make Nonstop Watches among the most accurate and reliable in the world, and these watches **6** .... (*expected*) **7** .... (*use*) as the official watches at the next Commonwealth Games. Next year, it **8** .... (*hope*) that a new completely automated factory **9** .... (*open*) and that all watches coming from the factory **10** .... (*manufacture*) by robots.

UNIT 16 Business meetings

Vocabulary

1 Use the words in the box to complete the note below.

action
agenda
attend
chair(person)
circulate
minutes

Amanda,
I've got to 1 .... an important meeting of the Advisory
Board tomorrow. Could you:
* find out who is going to be the 2 ....
* get hold of the 3 .... for me so I can prepare – and
make sure you 4 .... it to the other members of the board
* check that the 5 .... of the last meeting are typed up
* come in for 20 mins after lunch so we can check that all
the 6 .... points have been followed up.
Thanks
Sarah

2 a Combine a word from box A with a word from box B to make compound nouns which describe reasons for having meetings.

A

brain
decision
information
problem
team

B

building
sharing
solving
storming
making

b Complete these sentences using the compounds.

1 I know many of you think that email is a more efficient way of .... , but I can't be sure you read all your emails, so I thought I'd take this opportunity to tell you a few things.
2 Later today, we'll be holding a .... session to get ideas for new promotional activities.
3 Quite a number of the people have never worked together before, so the prime purpose of the meeting this afternoon is ....
4 We've discussed the issues at length on other occasions, so this meeting is primarily a .... meeting where we shall be taking the company in a new direction.
5 A number of difficulties have arisen in the production department, so today we're having a .... meeting to see if we can sort them out.

UNIT 16 Business meetings

3 Complete the crossword using verbs from page 74 of the Student's Book.

Across

2 I've decided to .... the meeting because it's not really necessary.
4 If you don't .... the meeting, you won't know what decisions are being taken.
6 Jane is ill, so I think we should .... the meeting until she's back at work.
7 It's all very well taking decisions, but who's going to .... them?

Down

1 Where are we going to .... the meeting? In the boardroom?
3 I've got too much work on my plate, so I think I'll .... this afternoon's meeting.
4 You're all looking pretty tired, so let's .... till after lunch.
5 Who's going to .... today's meeting? You, Susie?

Grammar

Write *too* or *enough* in each space.

1 We spent .... much time discussing the minutes from the last meeting.
2 They didn't allow .... time for the last point on the agenda.
3 The chairman wasn't firm .... with some of the people who attended.
4 I didn't get the agenda soon .... to be able to prepare for the meeting.
5 I think we have .... many meetings in this company.
6 There is just not .... space in the meeting room for all the people who have to attend.
7 If you speak .... quickly, people won't understand.
8 On the other hand, if you don't speak quickly ...., people get bored.

New technologies and change

Vocabulary

1 Which word in each group is the odd one out?

1 knowledge worker   skilled worker   blue-collar worker   professional
2 shift   switch   change   continue
3 grow   boost   downsize   increase
4 shortfall   accomplishment   gain   achievement
5 desktop   icon   screen   dotcom
6 customer   client   purchaser   supplier
7 probability   potential   capability   capacity

2 Choose the word or phrase, A, B, C or D, which best completes each sentence.

1 Our new CEO introduced a number of changes which laid the ...... for a complete transformation of our company.
   A basis   **B** groundwork   **C** start   **D** bottom
2 Our new computer facilities have enabled us to ...... our production process.
   A speed   **B** boost   **C** streamline   **D** quicken
3 We're hoping our new share offer will attract ....
   A investors   **B** spenders   **C** buyers   **D** speculators
4 This machine never breaks down – in fact, it's the most ...... in the factory.
   A trustworthy   **B** trusted   **C** faithful   **D** reliable
5 Our staff are totally ...... to making our company the best in the sector.
   A loyal   **B** focused   **C** committed   **D** convinced

Grammar

1 Complete the text by writing *a*, *an*, *the* or – (where you think no article is needed).

What the web taught FedEx

To understand how thoroughly **1** .... web has permeated **2** .... everyday business life, think back to **3** .... last time you tracked **4** .... package. Maybe you typed www.fedex.com into your browser. Or maybe you just pulled up **5** .... shipment information from **6** .... retailer's website.

That act, so normal today, was revolutionary ten years ago, when FedEx introduced **7** .... online package tracking. In November 1994, **8** .... web was **9** .... sea of static corporate brochures, with **10** .... messages from CEOs displayed on **11** .... grey pages. **12** .... idea that you could use **13** .... web for something that actually touched **14** .... real world was unheard of. **15** .... web has greatly increased **16** .... number of contacts **17** .... customers have with FedEx. But it's also cut FedEx's costs by $45 million **18** .... month, since **19** .... online tracking request costs 2 cents, vs. $2.40 for **20** .... phone call.

2 a Write sentences in your notebook about how business has changed using *used to*.

25 years ago	Now
1 Written communication: telex/letters	1 Written communication: email/fax
2 Computers: large mainframe computers	2 Computers: PCs and laptops
3 No Internet: companies mainly marketed regionally/nationally	3 Internet: companies can market globally
4 Business travel: expensive	4 Business travel: low-cost airlines
5 Spoken communication: fixed telephones / meetings	5 Spoken communication: mobile telephones / video conferencing / meetings
6 Information storage: paper based	6 Information storage: electronically based

1 Twenty-five years ago, written communication used to be done by telex or letters, but now it's done by email or faxes.

b Write three sentences of your own about how business has changed.

Reading

In most lines, there is one wrong word. Cross out the wrong word and write the correct word. If a line is correct, put a tick (✓).

~~While~~ I started working in an office, back in the mid-seventies, the	1 When
fax machine was still one thing of the future. Basically, we used to	2
rely on the postal service and the telephone, it was a monopoly and	3
therefore expensive and inefficient. To give you an idea of what it	4
was like, one day into my office I counted the number of times I	5
dialled a number and the number of times I get through. I found	6
that I dialled six times so often as I got through.	7
People didn't have computers on their desks. Computers were	8
enormous expensively machines which sat in basements and were	9
spoken about with great respect. Everything use to be typed by a	10
typist and of course correspondence took much long than it does	11
now.	

Writing

Write a short paragraph about how new technologies have changed the way you study or work.

Vocabulary

1 Use the words in the box to label the picture of a computer.

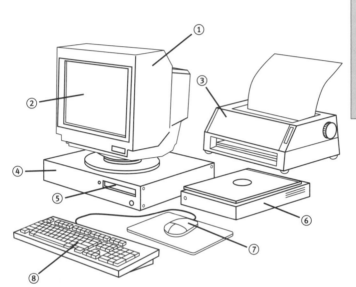

CD-ROM drive
CPU
keyboard
monitor
mouse
printer
scanner
screen

2 Write the correct word from the box in each space in the text below.

Isn't it marvellous that nowadays, with a few mouse **1** .... , you can **2** .... music or films from the Internet? Of course, it helps to have a fast **3** .... , otherwise doing this can take a really long time. Nowadays, of course, this is easy if you have a **4** .... connection. For people who have never done this, it's really easy. You go **5** .... and then you can either use a **6** .... , where you have to type in a word or two to say what you are looking for, or you can go to a portal, which will have all sorts of **7** .... to different websites where you can find the music or film that you want. Nowadays, these search engines and portals are very **8** ....– it's not difficult for anyone to use them, and the best websites are **9** .... almost everyday with the latest music or films available.

broadband
clicks
download
Internet
 connection
links
online
search engine
updated
user-friendly

Reading

1 Read the following email. In most lines there is one wrong word. Cross out the wrong word and write the correct word. If you think the line is correct, put a tick (✓).

To: Frank Lenz
Cc: Marina Laporte
Subject: Upgrading our website

Hello, Frank

Recently ~~us~~ company sales have been increasing quite rapidly here	1 our
in Europe, and for a result of our website, we are receiving enquiries	2
from customers in another parts of the world as well. These represent	3
a business opportunity what we ought to take advantage of.	4
We discuss this question at a meeting of the marketing personnel	5
yesterday, and decided that we should set off a facility for online	6
sales. We also decided that our website should be available in other	7
languages apart of English and French. We thought that it should	8
also be translated into Spanish and Chinese.	9
Could it be possible for you to upgrade our website in the ways	10
I have suggested, and could you give me a quotation for how much	11
it would cost to carry on this work?	12
If you require further informations, please call me on 964 538729 (direct line).	13

Best wishes

Nicole Crété

2 Read the following text about spam (direct mail using the Internet) and write one word in each space.

Spam is not a new problem. It was identified 20 years **1** .... But it is getting worse. While in the traditional Internet culture practically everyone agreed **2** .... was wrong, now some people **3** .... to think that it is a good idea, especially **4** .... a tool for business. They are wrong: it is not doing **5** .... good for business online. Some large companies now are quite concerned **6** .... of the floods of spam that **7** .... interfering with their email and confusing their organisation. **8** .... have been several attempts to stop spamming, or at least reduce it, but **9** .... far they have failed. Some authorities (including the European Union) have acknowledged the problem, but with **10** .... practical results. Laws are likely to do more harm **11** .... good. They could interfere with Net freedom, create unnecessary bureaucracy, while leaving **12** .... spam problem unsolved.

19 A staff survey

Vocabulary

1 Complete the text with a word or phrase from the box.

| absenteeism |
| bonus scheme |
| long hours |
| motivated |
| off sick |
| productivity |
| staff retention |
| staff turnover |
| work-life |

Making staff happy

May Electronics had a problem of **1** .... , with many staff phoning in to say they were sick. Also, although they paid high wages, workers did not seem to stay with them long, and **2** .... was almost 20% a year. Eventually, the managing director, Sophie May, decided to call in a consultant, who reached the conclusion that most staff were under too much stress. Many complained that they worked **3** .... and that, as a result, they were unable to have a reasonable **4** .... balance. Also, many felt that management did not value their work, and, as a result, they did not feel **5** .... to work very hard. The fact that workers were doing their jobs slowly and were frequently **6** .... with colds, back pain and headaches affected **7** .... , so that less was being produced per working day than ten years ago. The consultant recommended that Sophie should introduce a **8** .... , so that workers were paid extra for being more productive. Also, he suggested that a more flexible working system would help **9** .... and mean fewer people leaving the company.

2 Choose the best alternative, A, B or C, for each sentence.

1 Only 2% of our customers complain, so in comparison with our satisfied customers, they are a ....
   A limited number   **B** tiny minority   **C** significant number

2 The .... of banks, 95% in fact, increased their profits last year.
   A vast majority   **B** growing numbers   **C** significant number

3 Internet use is becoming increasingly popular amongst older people – the 'silver surfers' as they are known – and .... of them are buying online (25% of customers last year as opposed to 15% the year before).
   A a smaller percentage   **B** a limited number   **C** growing numbers

4 At the Annual General Meeting, Bill Ashley was elected with a .... of the votes – nearly 65%.
   A growing number   **B** substantial majority   **C** vast majority

5 A .... of people, perhaps as much as 35%, said they would be interested in buying our product.
   A significant number   **B** limited number   **C** growing number

3 Make nouns from these adjectives (in some cases you can make more than one noun).

1 expensive ...expense....   4 stressful   7 efficient
2 flexible   5 absent   8 modern
3 productive   6 motivated   9 relaxing

Grammar

1 Read these sentences, which are in reported speech, then write the original words which the speaker used in your notebook.

1 He told me he was going to book his flight online
  'I'm going to book my flight online.'
2 She said she worked for a bank in New York.
3 Marcelle told Sheila she had never worked in accounts before.
4 Danielle said she had already printed out the sales forecast.
5 Leo said he would fix the meeting for three o'clock the next day.
6 Maxine said she couldn't speak to me because she was busy.
7 Caroline told me they might change the computer system the following year.
8 Kamal said they had bought new software the previous month.
9 He said that the sales figures were bad.

2 In your notebook, put these sentences into reported speech using the reporting verb given in brackets.

1 'Oil prices are going to fall,' said the minister. (*predicted*)
  The minister predicted that oil prices were going to fall.
2 'Go to Berlin on the next plane,' said my boss. (*ordered*)
3 'There has been a 3% drop in market share,' I told them. (*informed*)
4 'Would you mind phoning the suppliers?' she said to Helga. (*requested*)
5 'When can you deliver the goods?' I asked her. (*enquired*)
6 'I'll have that report on your desk by midday tomorrow,' I told my boss. (*promised*)
7 'We don't know how much the development costs will be,' said the project leader. (*answered*)

3 Each of these sentences has one mistake. Rewrite them correctly.

1 He said me he would give me a discount.
  He told me he would give me a discount. / He said he would give me a discount.
2 He told to me that the package had been sent the day before.
3 She explained him that she would prefer flexible working to part-time working.
4 He answered that he had changed jobs the last year.
5 She asked him how much did the flights cost.
6 He promised me that he will send the goods last week.
7 The caller enquired when would the product be launched.
8 He explained that he has forgotten to send the invoice.
9 He ordered her that she signed the cheque for $10,000.
10 I told him to not send the application by email.

20 Offshoring and outsourcing

Vocabulary

1 a Match the verbs (1–6) with the nouns (a–f) to form business collocations.

1	generate	a	an economic downturn
2	make ... redundant	b	back-office functions
3	undergo	c	exposure to risk
4	face	d	fierce competition
5	outsource	e	profits
6	reduce	f	staff

b Complete these sentences with the collocations you formed in Exercise 1a, putting the verb in the correct form.

1 By .... such as the payroll to a specialist company, we could save time and money.

2 In reality, we regard outsourcing as a way of .... , since we would not have to close factories if there was an economic downturn.

3 One of the main responsibilities of a marketing manager is to .... for his company.

4 Raising interest rates would lead to the country .... , and this would certainly affect our sales and eat into our profits.

5 We .... from companies in other parts of Asia who are able to produce similar products at two-thirds the price.

6 We thought that our headquarters was heavily overstaffed and we realised that by .... , we could reduce our salary bill.

2 Complete the following sentences by choosing the best answer, A, B, C or D.

1 We're introducing an incentive scheme as part of an effort to reduce staff ....
   A retention   **B** turnover   **C** shifts   **D** changes

2 Baxters have about 1,000 workers in the factory at ...... times, which means that things are very crowded.
   A peak   **B** top   **C** high   **D** maximum

3 The Human Resources Department has decided to ...... with plans to reduce sick leave among workers.
   A go off   **B** go up   **C** go on   **D** go ahead

4 A survey amongst staff ...... has revealed dissatisfaction with their working hours.
   A people   **B** members   **C** workers   **D** employees

5 We can outsource a lot of routine administrative work, but there are some ...... activities which we have to keep in-house.
   A prime   **B** first   **C** core   **D** central

6 With our company ...... increasing competition from other countries, we
need to become more efficient.
A confronting   B opposing   C fighting   D facing
7 The chairman told a meeting of shareholders that profits would reach a ......
level this year.
A top   B best   C record   D highest
8 With such fierce competition and rising costs, we may find our ...... margins
are affected.
A benefit   B profit   C revenue   D earnings

Reading

You work for an import agency in your country. Read the following letter
from a UK company. In most lines there is one extra word. However, some
lines are correct. Write the extra word. If the line is correct, put a tick (✓).

Dear Sir or Madam,	
We are a producer of top-quality frozen fish and vegetables ~~being~~	1 being
based in Felixstowe, England. Our customers do consist of large retail	2
chains and are leading supermarkets throughout the United Kingdom.	3
At present time, we are investigating the possibility of expanding	4
our export market and we are wondering what potential your	5
country has made for our products. We would be interested in	6
selling to supermarkets and could offer a very competitive prices.	7
You will find enclosed a brochure is giving details of our products.	8
I would be grateful if you could to tell us:	9
1 if do you think there is a market for our products in your country	10
2 whether you would be interested in acting as an import agent	11
and distributor on our behalf.	12
I am also considering visiting to your country next March in order	13
to do some fact-finding. During my visit, I would be welcome	14
an opportunity to meet you. Can you suggest giving some suitable	15
dates in March month for a visit?	16
I look forward to hearing from you.	
Yours faithfully,	
Jonathan Barraclough	
Export Manager	

Writing

Write an answer to the letter above.
• Say that you are interested.
• Explain there is a market.
• Suggest dates for a meeting.

21 Customer loyalty

Vocabulary

Read the following text. For each gap, choose the best word, A, B, C or D.

As every manager knows, 'the customer comes 1 ....' and 'the customer is always right'. Despite these phrases being repeated so often, it is remarkable how many organisations 2 .... essential training in customer care. All too frequently when 3 .... front-office staff, customers are met with rudeness, lack of interest or 4 .... of stress, and these all give a negative 5 .... of the organisation itself. Many customers have come to 6 .... treatment of this kind, and as a 7 .... behave aggressively or irritably themselves. These customers very often are the 'awkward customers' whom even well-trained customer service staff find hard to 8 .... Many experts believe that not 9 .... in an organisation has the right personality for a customer-service position and that this should be taken into 10 .... when recruiting front-line staff. Even with training, some people will never have the people 11 .... to deal successfully with customers in what can be a very stressful 12 .... There are also a number of experts who advocate training for customers in how to 13 .... the best out of the staff they have to deal with. However, this would only really be 14 .... in company-to-company situations where, for instance, company buyers have to deal with people from a 15 .... of different suppliers.

1 **A** top	**B** first	**C** best	**D** ahead
2 **A** abandon	**B** stop	**C** neglect	**D** drop
3 **A** approaching	**B** reaching	**C** arriving	**D** talking
4 **A** signals	**B** indications	**C** signs	**D** appearances
5 **A** view	**B** opinion	**C** idea	**D** impression
6 **A** expect	**B** wait	**C** hope	**D** worry
7 **A** result	**B** feedback	**C** principle	**D** summary
8 **A** deal	**B** treat	**C** look	**D** handle
9 **A** anyone	**B** someone	**C** no one	**D** everyone
10 **A** thought	**B** account	**C** granted	**D** advantage
11 **A** skills	**B** knowledge	**C** abilities	**D** capabilities
12 **A** location	**B** work	**C** appointment	**D** post
13 **A** obtain	**B** take	**C** extract	**D** get
14 **A** able	**B** capable	**C** practical	**D** competent
15 **A** quantity	**B** number	**C** amount	**D** selection

Grammar

1 Write the correct relative pronoun in each space in the following email. You can leave the space blank if no pronoun is necessary.

⬤ ⬤ ⬤	In	⬤

Hello, Sam

Do you remember the customer **1** ...... called from Odessa last month? Well, she has just called again to complain that the tool **2** ...... we sent her was not the one **3** ...... she ordered. She says that **4** ...... she wanted was the OH200, not the OH300. Andrew wants to know who is responsible for this. You are the one **5** ...... handwriting is on the order form, and in the space **6** ...... you have to write the product type, you have written OH200, but very indistinctly, and that could be the reason **7** ...... the order was mixed up.

8 ...... you need to do is:
• explain to Andrew, **9** ...... is pretty angry I warn you.
• sort the thing out with the customer in Odessa – I suggest you send a replacement tool by those express couriers **10** ...... number is on the notice board.

Thanks

Mary

2 Join these sentences by using relative clauses.

1 There's a man on the phone. He says he spoke to you yesterday.

....

2 Did you repair the computer? It wasn't working.

....

3 I phoned the customer. His invoice hadn't arrived.

....

4 We stayed at an excellent hotel. It was near the city centre.

....

5 I work for a software company. Its headquarters are in Silicon Valley.

....

6 Have you visited the factory? They make the components there.

....

7 Claudio is the technician. He knows how to install the equipment.

....

8 We'll hold the meeting at 11 o'clock. Everyone is free then.

....

9 You forgot to answer the letter. I wrote it.

....

22 Communication with customers

Grammar

Complete each of these sentences with a preposition.

1 Her company has a commitment ....to.... giving good service.
2 If you're dissatisfied .... the service, you ought to complain.
3 Few customers ever complain .... the price of our products.
4 She tries to build long-term relationships .... her clients.
5 One of his duties is to take care .... customer relationships.
6 I'm responsible .... updating the company website.
7 Our employees show tremendous loyalty .... the company.
8 What methods do you have for communicating .... your customers?
9 The best way .... keeping your customers is by exceeding their expectations.
10 We have been successfully competing .... two much larger companies for more than ten years.
11 You should focus .... the clients who spend the most money.
12 His irresponsible behaviour resulted .... a commercial disaster.

Reading

In most lines of this email there is one wrong word. Cross out the wrong word and write the correct word. If you think the line is correct, Put a tick (✓).

Dear Mrs Fenton,

I am writing to you ~~like~~ a valued and long-standing client of ours (your	1 *as*
company has been outsourcing your printing requirements to us since	2
the past 15 years).	3
I am delighted to be able to inform you for some innovations we have	4
been introducing in our way of making business with you. As from now,	5
if you wish, you will have access to a dedicated extranet who links	6
ExtraPrint with our most important clients. All you will have to do	7
is post some printing job you require on the extranet, together with	8
your instructions on how it should been printed, and we will do the	9
job for you almost immediately. For no extra cost, the completed work	10
will be delivered to you by express courier. You will be invoiced	11
electronic at the same time.	12
Please let me know if this new service interesting you, and I will	13
be delighted to call you for explain it in more detail, or to visit you	14
at a time which is convenient for you.	15

Yours sincerely,

Writing

1 Study the chart and the handwritten notes. Then complete the sales report below by writing one word from the phrases expressing causes which you have studied in each space.

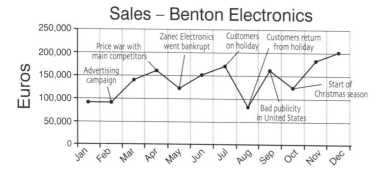

Sales – Benton Electronics

Report on sales: Benton Electronics

Our sales from January to February stayed the same at €90,000. However, in March, **1** .... to our advertising campaign, sales increased by €50,000 to reach a level of €140,000. This trend continued in April, with sales of €160,000. Unfortunately, between April and May, we had a price war with our competitors, and this **2** .... in a fall in sales of €40,000. However, during May, our competitor, Zanec, went bankrupt, and this **3** .... to an increase over the next two months of €50,000.

At the end of July, most of our customers went on holiday, and this **4** .... a fall in sales of €90,000. However, when they returned in September, sales recovered, reaching a level of €160,000. As a **5** .... of bad publicity in the US in September, our sales for October dropped to €120,000, but **6** .... to the Christmas season, they recovered to reach €200,000 in December.

---

2 Write a sales report for Carmel Sun Creams. Use the information on the chart and the handwritten notes. Use the report in Exercise 1 as a model.

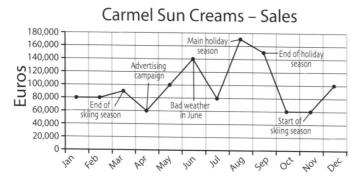

Carmel Sun Creams – Sales

Vocabulary

1 a Match the verbs (1–8) with the noun or noun phrases (a–h) to form collocations.

1	extend	a	a face-to-face meeting
2	charge	b	construction work
3	do	c	costs
4	carry out	d	high prices
5	organise	e	our range of services
6	meet	f	your requirements
7	calculate	g	trouble-free business
8	organise	h	work schedules

b Complete each of these sentences with a collocation from Exercise 1a.

1 Although they .charge high prices. , there is no doubt that their services offer value for money.

2 I hope the services we offer will .... and that we will be able to add you to our long list of satisfied customers.

3 I'm fed up with discussing all these things over the phone. I think we should .... as soon as possible.

4 Our excellent range of video-conferencing equipment will help you to .... from anywhere in your building.

5 The building company is arriving tomorrow to .... on the other side of the staff car park.

6 The work is very complex, so it's very hard to .... exactly. However, we will try to produce the most competitive estimate we can.

7 We have decided to .... by including accounting and auditing among the things we do.

8 With so many new projects starting, it's difficult to .... so that everyone is occupied and no one has too much work to do.

2 Complete these sentences with the correct form of the words shown in brackets.

1 We prefer to concentrate our efforts on .existing. customers rather than look for new ones. (*exist*)

2 Bad publicity from .... customers can be very damaging to a firm. (*satisfy*)

3 Please allow seven days from placing the order to date of .... (*deliver*)

4 The report is .... , so don't leave it lying around on your desk – lock it in a drawer. (*confident*)

5 Mallory's service is pretty .... – you never know when they're going to deliver the goods. (*rely*)

6 Doing this job by hand is so .... compared with doing it by machine. It wastes a lot of time. (*efficient*)

7 He has an .... network of contacts who can help him whenever he has a problem. (*extend*)

8 Our products give .... results, so I'm sure you'll be one of our many satisfied customers. (*guarantee*)

9 As a .... long-standing customer, we would like you to take advantage of this special offer. (*value*)

3 a Match the beginnings of the phrases (1–7) with their endings (a–g) to make some typical phrases used in business letters.

1	I would be most grateful	a	enclosed our ...
2	I am writing	b	hearing ...
3	Following our telephone	c	I am writing to ...
	conversation this morning,	d	if you could send me ...
4	With reference to	e	to inform you that ...
5	Thank you	f	for your letter of 18 March enquiring about ...
6	I look forward to	g	your suggestion ...
7	Please find		

b Complete the phrases to form a sentence you might find in a business letter.

Grammar

In your notebook, express the following causes and results using the words given in brackets.

1 Our printer ran out of ink and we had to address all the letters by hand. (*meant*)

Our printer ran out of ink, and this meant us having to address all the letters by hand.

OR Our printer ran out of ink and this meant that we had to address all the letters by hand.

2 Unfortunately, Central Europe was hit by heavy storms last week, and we have fallen behind with our deliveries. (*consequence*)

3 There was a power cut in our area last week. Our computer system was put out of operation. (*meant*)

4 Our suppliers were late sending us some components. We were unable to complete your order on time. (*result*)

5 I am pleased to inform you that our suppliers have given us a considerable discount. We are in a position to offer you the goods you have ordered at a reduced price. (*consequently*)

6 Unfortunately, my secretary copied your telephone number incorrectly. I was unable to contact you. (*meant*)

Vocabulary

1 Choose the best word, A, B, C or D, for each gap.

1 The successful candidate for this post will probably be ...... externally.

 A contracted **B** engaged **C** taken on **D** recruited

2 We will have to work through the weekend in order to meet the ...... we've been set.

 A bottom line **B** last time **C** deadline **D** final hour

3 You should inform your superior as soon as possible if you think you are going to have difficulty in ...... targets.

 A meeting **B** finding **C** arriving **D** getting

4 I've been busy this week working on the annual sales ....

 A prediction **B** forecast **C** preview **D** prevision

5 They have put the new product on ...... in their showroom.

 A exhibition **B** display **C** sight **D** exposure

6 We have sent free ...... of the product to all our most important customers.

 A samples **B** examples **C** instances **D** shows

7 The recent advertising ...... was designed to boost brand awareness.

 A battle **B** war **C** fight **D** campaign

8 Connex and Passley have been waging a fierce price ...... in an effort to increase market share.

 A battle **B** war **C** fight **D** campaign

9 This is not the typical consumer product which will appeal to everyone, but there should be a ...... market for it.

 A special **B** tight **C** reserved **D** niche

10 Drenden Pty Ltd will be ...... as our agents in Australia.

 A working **B** performing **C** acting **D** playing

11 Customer service is what gives the company a(n) ...... over the competition.

 A edge **B** side **C** line **D** border

12 It's important to keep ...... to a minimum if you are going to make a decent profit.

 A oversights **B** overheads **C** overalls **D** overwork

13 We expect retailers to add a 100% ...... on our products when they sell them.

 A margin **B** extra **C** addition **D** mark-up

2 Choose the best word, A, B, C or D, for each gap.

1 When he needed to raise a loan, he used his ...... such as his house as security.

   A assets   **B** liabilities   **C** turnover   **D** fixtures

2 Many products ...... because companies haven't done market research before developing them.

   A fall   **B** sink   **C** drop   **D** fail

3 The interest ...... has been raised to 5% this week.

   A rate   **B** type   **C** cost   **D** percentage

4 It's been a pleasure ...... business with you.

   A making   **B** having   **C** running   **D** doing

5 Entrepreneurs are people who enjoy ...... risks.

   A making   **B** having   **C** taking   **D** doing

6 Unless turnover increases, he'll never ...... his start-up loan.

   A pay up   **B** pay off   **C** pay in   **D** pay out

7 The posters will need to have good visual ...... if they are going to be effective.

   A impact   **B** strike   **C** impression   **D** hit

8 Doing the VAT returns is a very time-...... task.

   A using   **B** consuming   **C** spending   **D** wasting

9 Don't bother to copy down these figures because I'm going to ...... a photocopy at the end.

   A hand out   **B** give in   **C** deal with   **D** enter

10 Our respondents ...... quality of service as the most important thing in the survey.

   A evaluated   **B** assessed   **C** appraised   **D** rated

11 Poor quality control is unlikely to ...... the company's image.

   A enhance   **B** better   **C** grow   **D** reform

12 Martin has a proven track ...... as an outstanding speaker.

   A background   **B** reputation   **C** curriculum   **D** record

13 By the end of this year, our debts should have ...... to less than 10% of turnover.

   A lowered   **B** reduced   **C** cut   **D** decreased

14 To start this meeting, I'm going to ask the company secretary to read the ...... of our previous meeting.

   A agenda   **B** minutes   **C** points   **D** notes

15 It took us years to ...... the solution to our production problems.

   A come out with   **B** come in for   **C** come up with   **D** come about

16 He ...... the export department in our company.

   A works   **B** runs   **C** does   **D** makes

17 One of the problems with taking legal action is that lawyers' ...... are so high.

   A salaries   **B** fees   **C** charges   **D** payments

Word list

Some of these words appear in the transcripts at the end of the Student's Book. U= unit, T = track, so *U1 T1* means Unit 1 Track 1.

A

abreast: keep abreast of (p 114) stay informed about the most recent facts

absenteeism *n* (p 90) people taking time off work when they should be there

academic background *n* (p 21) what you have studied and the qualifications you have received

accident: is no accident (p 65) has been planned for carefully

accounting *n* (p 14) activity of preparing and maintaining financial records

across the spectrum (U18 T1) including the widest possible range of people

action point *n* (p 76) thing assigned to specific person to be achieved before the next meeting

address *v* (p 69) deal with

adjourn *v* (p 76) stop a meeting temporarily with the intention of continuing it at a later time

after-sales service *n* (p 106) help or advice received after a purchase has been made

agent *n* (p 57) company which sells another company's products on commission

anecdote *n* (p 115) short, amusing story

angel investor *n* (U10 T18) private investor willing to invest money in new businesses

appeals to *v* (p 83) interests

application *n* (U10 T18) computer program designed for a particular purpose

appraisal *n* (p 13) assessment or evaluation of how well you do your job

areas *pl n* (p 16) departments

audit *v* (p 16) check that financial statements and accounts are correct

B

baby: your own baby *n* (U2 T3) project or piece of work that you care about a lot because it was your idea

bankrupt *adj* (p 67) having no money; unable to continue in business because you cannot pay your debts

bear in mind *v* (U13 T22) remember when making plans

behind the scenes (U14 T25) which the public don't see or meet

benchmark *n* (p 113) high level of quality which can be used as a standard when comparing other things

best practice *n* (p 100) best way of working

bid *n* (p 67) the price offered for a piece of work or a service

billion *n* (p 83) one thousand million (1,000,000,000)

bioinformatics *n* (p 55) information science about living things

board of directors *n* (p 16) top-level managers of a company

bond *n* (p 101) relationship

bonus scheme *n* (p 10) company system in which employees receive extra payments if certain targets are reached

book-keeping *n* (p 10) recording the money that an organisation or business spends and receives

boom *v* (U14 T25) grow rapidly and successfully

bottom line *n* (p 65) the most important thing

brand awareness *n* (p 29) knowledge among people in general that a certain brand exists

branding *n* (p 28) giving a company or product a particular design or symbol in order to give it an identity for marketing and advertising purposes

break the bank *v* (p 67) allow something to cost more than you can afford

brief *n* (U22 T8) set of instructions

bring up details *v* (p 23) find information on a computer

brochure *n* (p 28) magazine published by a company advertising or giving information about its products or services

browse *v* (p 86) search the Internet

budget *n* (p 38) money you have available to spend

bulk: in bulk *adj* (p 43) in large quantities

bulletin *n* (p 104) short, written news update

business card *n* (p 53) small card to give to business contacts showing your name, job title and details of the company you work for

business case *n* (p 101) the real value to the business

business centre *n* (p 64) facilities that business people can use to do work or contact people, e.g. fax machines, secretarial help, Internet connections

business culture *n* (p 102) the beliefs and way of behaving of a particular company

buy into *v* (U9 T16) invest in

buzz *n* (U14 T25) feeling of excitement

C

call off *v* (p 76) cancel

candidate *n* (p 17) person applying for a job

capitalise on *v* (p 29) benefit from, take advantage of

carry a lot of stock *v* (p 42) keep a large amount of stock in a shop / chain of shops

cashflow *n* (p 35) the amount of money moving through a business

cashier *n* (p 17) the person who takes the money when customers pay at a supermarket

catch on *v* (U10 T18) become popular

centrepiece *n* (p 29) the most important or attractive part or feature of something

CEO *n* (p 14) short for **Chief Executive Officer**

chain *n* (p 65) number of businesses owned by the same company

chair *v* (p 76) direct or manage a meeting

challenging *adj* (p 17) difficult and demanding to do

checkout *n* (U2 T4) the place in a supermarket where you pay for your shopping

Chief Executive Officer *n* (p 14) highest manager with responsibility for the day-to-day running of a company

Chief Information Officer *n* (p 14) manager responsible for information and computer systems

chill-out zone *n* (U6 T11) area for people to relax in

CIO *n* (p 14) short for **Chief Information Officer**

classified ad *n* (p 83) small advertisement usually placed by private individuals or small companies

clear up *v* (U11 T20) deal with, get an explanation for

click *v* (p 86) press the mouse button

cloned *adj* (p 55) plant or animal which has the same genes as the original from which it was produced artificially

co-founder *n* (p 33) person you begin a company with

cold-call *v* (U10 T17) phone or visit possible clients to try and sell something without any previous contact or an appointment

come back to you on that *v* (U8 T14) talk to you again in order to give you further information

comment card *n* (U21 T6) card on which customers write their opinions and suggestions

commitment *n* (p 106) willingness to give time and energy

common sense *n* (U3 T5) practical, sensible thinking and judgement

competition *n* (U9 T16) other companies which produce the same goods or services as your company

competitive advantage *n* (p 101) having an advantage over your competitors by being better than them

competitive differentiation *n* (p 102) the special things about a company's products that make them different from those of other companies

computer literate *adj* (p 12) able to use a computer competently

confidence: have confidence in someone (p 102) trust someone's abilities

consumer product *n* (p 21) product bought by the public and not by companies

contacts *pl n* (p 35) people, especially in high positions, who can give you useful information or introductions which will help you at work

core *n* (p 12) central, essential

cost-effective *adj* (p 94) of good value to you for the amount of money paid

coverage: brilliant coverage *n* (p 173) excellent reports in both quantity and quality

credit facilities *pl n* (p 49) arrangement to borrow or owe money in order to buy goods

critical *adj* (p 25) very important

cross-fertilisation of ideas *n* (U11 T20) mixing of ideas from different types of people to stimulate new thinking

customer base *n* (U6 T10) regular customers

customer care *n* (p 105) the way customers are treated

customer profile *n* (p 114) description of an average customer

customer relations *pl n* (p 14) approach to management which recognises the value of building and maintaining a long-term relationship with customers through, e.g. special credit cards, loyalty cards

customer service *n* (p 17) giving customers good service

customer services manager *n* (p 106) person responsible for before- and after-sales service

customised *adj* (p 33) made especially to suit the user's needs

cutbacks *pl n* (p 93) reductions made in order to save money

CV *n* (p 21) short for **curriculum vitae**: a written summary of work experience and qualifications sent to a possible employer by someone applying for a job

cyberspace *n* (p 83) the imaginary place where Internet data exists

D

date: to date (p 85) up to the present time

dating skills *pl n* (p 29) ability to begin a romantic relationship

deadline *n* (p 14) final time by which a task or job must be completed

dealership *n* (p 101) business that sells the products of a particular company, e.g. car dealership

decent *adj* (p 33) good

dedicated *adj* (p 11) designed especially for that use

defy a conventional business plan *v* (U10 T18) be too difficult to explain in a normal business plan

degree *n* (p 13) university qualification

deli *n* (U6 T9) small shop that sells high-quality foods, such as types of cheese and cold cooked meat, which often come from other countries

deliberate *v* (p 109) think carefully about something

deliver *v* (p 38) provide what was promised

desktop *n* (p 85) software program where icons and files are displayed on a computer screen

details: bring up your details *v* (p 23) find information about you on my computer

digest *v* (p 60) take time to understand

direct mail *n* (p 29) publicity sent directly to a person's home

discount the job *v* (U22 T8) reduce the price

distributor *n* (p 57) company which buys another company's products and sells them in a particular region

domestic *adj* (p 94) from within the same country

door-to-door *adj* (p 109) all the stages of a journey from the beginning to the end

the dot-com crash *n* (p 85) period when there was fast growth in dot-com companies. A dot-com company is one that sells goods and services through the Internet. The projected income of many companies never materialised, and a lot of shareholders' money was lost in a short space of time.

down *adj* (U18 T2) not working, disconnected for a time

download *v* (p 86) transfer information from the Internet to a computer

drawback *n* (p 28) disadvantage

dream up *v* (p 31) invent

drive *v* (p 101) work hard to produce

drop an email *v* (p 70) send a short, quick email

drop the idea *v* (p 47) decide not to continue

dry up *v* (p 60) have nothing more to say

E

e-commerce *n* (p 83) the activity of selling goods or services through the Internet

eco-tourism *n* (p 69) tourism connected with the environment and nature

edge *n* (p 38) advantage

emerging market *n* (p 69) new or developing market

empowerment *n* (p 101) giving employees responsibility so that they have the power to make their own decisions in their job

engaged *adj* (p 101) involved and interested

enhance *v* (p 69) improve

entrepreneur *n* (U9 T16) person who starts up a new business

entrepreneurial skills *pl n* (p 33) abilities connected with starting a new business

entrepreneurship *n* (p 69) the starting up of new businesses

essence *n* (p 31) most important quality

estate agencies *n* (p 47) businesses that arrange the selling, renting or management of property and land for their owners

event tourism *n* (p 181) holidays taken not just to visit a place but also for the special events happening there

expense: at the expense of (U20 T5) at the same time having a negative effect on

eye contact: make eye contact *v* (p 60) look at people's eyes to keep them involved

F

failure rate *n* (p 47) the number which do not succeed

fat cat *n* (U9 T16) someone who has a lot of money and who has the power to increase their own income

feature *v* (p 113) include as an important part

fee *n* (p 47) money you pay for professional services

feel free to *v* (p 59) don't be afraid to

Finance Manager *n* (p 14) the manager responsible for the accounting and financial affairs of a company

financial year n (p 16) the 12-month period for which a company produces accounts

findings pl n (U12 T21) information discovered

fingertips: at your fingertips (U18 T2) available for immediate use

fire v (p 17) dismiss someone from their job

firm n (p 13) company

first: in the first place (p 46) at the start

first-come-first-serve (U7 T12) dealt with in the order in which people ask

flying start n (p 12) very good beginning

focus group n (p 31) group of people who are paid to discuss and give their opinions for market research

forecast v (p 16) predict business and financial performance for the future

formula n (p 69) combination of things which will produce the result you want

found v (p 33) set up or establish a company or organisation

found out adj (U3 T5) shown to be dishonest

franchise n (p 46) right to sell a company's products in a particular location using the company's name

frequent-flier program (UK **programme**) n (p 65) system where regular users of an airline earn points to get benefits and discounts

FT n (U6 T11) a commonly used abbreviation for the *Financial Times*, an important British newspaper for people who are interested in finance, business and economics, printed on pink paper

fulfilling adj (U2 T3) making you happy or satisfied

full-on adj (p 19) total

G

gadget n (p 42) small device or machine with a particular purpose

gap in the market n (p 33) opportunity to sell a new product which isn't being sold already

gathering n (p 67) large group meeting

generic adj (U6 T9) relating to a group of similar things rather than one thing in particular

get a feel for v (U24 T10) develop a good knowledge or understanding of

get at v (U18 T1) find, locate

get down to v (U11 T20) start

get in v (U8 T13) arrive

get off the ground v (U10 T18) start

get onto v (U11 T20) start dealing with

get round to it v (U14 T24) do what you've intended to do

get together v (U16 T27) organise, produce

gift n (p 28) something which is given to you

gig n (p 19) performance, concert

go about v (U3 T5) start dealing with

go from strength to strength v (U9 T16) become increasingly successful

go it alone v (p 47) start your own business

go straight in the bin *v* (U3 T5) be thrown away without being looked at

goal *n* (p 11) aim, objective, target

government grant *n* (p 52) money given by the government for a special purpose

graduate *n* (p 13) someone who has obtained a university degree

graduation *n* (p 16) the moment of successfully completing one's university course

great deal *n* (p 25) a lot

great stuff (*inf*) (U11 T20) 'That's excellent!'

ground-breaking *adj* (p 54) new and very different from others of its type

gush *v* (p 65) express so strongly that it does not sound sincere

gut instinct *n* (U10 T18) strong belief which cannot be explained

H

hand: old hand *n* (p 180) very experienced person

hands-on *adj* (p 12) practical, not theoretical

hang on *v* (inf) (p 23) wait a moment

hardware *n* (p 83) computer equipment or machinery (as opposed to software)

hassle *n* (U24 T10) trouble

have something to do with *v* (p 50) be connected with

help desk *n* (p 106) place customers can visit or phone when they have problems

helpline *n* (p 106) telephone service for when customers have problems

high flier *n* (p 11) someone with a lot of ability and ambition who is expected to be successful

hit *n* (p 29) time when someone visits a website

hi-tech *adj* (p 52) using the most modern and advanced machines and technology

hoist *n* (p 110) machine used for lifting heavy things

home page *n* (p 86) first/front page of a website

household name *n* (p 47) company name that most people have heard of

HRM *n* (p 14) short for **Human Resources Manager**

Human Resources Manager *n* (p 14) the manager responsible for recruiting, training and managing employees

hush-hush *adj* (U11 T20) secret

hype *v* (p 30) publicise strongly, advertise in an exaggerated way

I

icon *n* (p 87) small picture or symbol on a computer screen that you click on to open a program

implement *v* (p 90) put into operation

implementation *n* (p 69) putting something into action

implication *n* (U14 T24) possible effect

incentive event *n* (U2 T3) conference or other event which companies use for thanking customers and rewarding their staff

information-rich site *n* (p 88) site which people visit mainly for the information it contains

in-house *adj* (p 10) taking place within the company

innovation *n* (p 18) new idea or product

insight *n* (p 70) understanding

intended recipient *n* (p 25) the person you wanted to contact

interior designer *n* (p 47) person who plans the decoration of the inside of a building

interviewee *n* (p 17) person being interviewed

intractable *adj* (U14 T24) seemingly impossible to solve

intranets *n* (U20 T4) systems of connected computers within organisations through which employees can communicate with each other and share information

IT *n* (p 16) short for Information Technology; computer and telecommunications technology

itchy fingers *pl n* (p 88) people who will quickly leave your website and go to another one if they don't find it interesting and quick to use

J

Javascript *n* (p 88) a computer programming language frequently used on the Internet

job satisfaction *n* (p 18) feeling of pleasure and achievement in your job

junk *adj* (U18 T2) information sent to people, although they do not want it and have not asked for it, usually advertising products or services

justify *v* (p 95) provide a good enough reason

K

keen *adj* (p 38) competitive

keep abreast of *v* (p 114) stay informed about the most recent facts

keep momentum *v* (p 35) keep something developing after it has started

keep up with *v* (U11 T20) not fall behind

key *adj* (p 11) very important, essential

keynote speaker *n* (p 66) the most important speaker at a conference

kiosk *n* (p 19) small building where products are sold

knowledge: to my knowledge (U18 T1) as far as I know

knowledge industry *n* (p 55) service industry in which employees deal in knowledge rather than products and need a high level of education and training

knowledge worker *n* (p 85) person whose job requires a high level of education and training

L

label *n* (p 33) company name or symbol

launch *v* (p 14) start selling a product or service for the first time

leaflet *n* (p 28) printed material of a page or a few pages publicising or giving information about a product or service

learning goals: meet the learning goals v (p 12) provide good enough instruction in what the employees want to learn

leave high and dry v (U20 T5) put in a difficult and inconvenient situation which it is difficult to get out of

legitimate adj (p 47) likely and reasonable

liaise v (p 38) communicate and exchange information

lifestyle n, adj (U2 T3) the way that you live your life

limited adj (p 11) company where each shareholder is responsible for the company's debts up to but no more than the amount that he/she has invested in the company

line: new line n (p 33) new type of product

loan n (p 51) money which is lent or borrowed

log off v (p 88) close down a computer

log on v (p 30) start using a computer; (p 65) visit a website

logo n (p 31) design which represents a company or a product

long-standing adj (p 109) for a long time

lottery n (p 29) game in which numbered tickets are sold to people who then have a chance of winning a prize if their number is chosen

loved one n (U18 T1) person that you love, usually a member of your family

loyalty program n (p 65) reward system, e.g. free hotel breaks to thank regular customers for buying goods and services from a business

M

machine tool n (p 90) tool which uses power to cut and shape strong materials

mail order n (p 107) buying goods, usually from a catalogue, by post

make a go of v (U9 T16) make successful by working hard

make do v (U10 T17) use what was available

make it v (p 182) be present

make redundant v (U9 T16) fire someone because their job is no longer needed

make the most of v (p 60) take full advantage of an opportunity which will not last long

man v (p 36) be present at, help to run

man hour n (p 111) the amount of work one person can do in an hour

management accounting n (p 16) preparing financial information to help management decisions

Managing Director n (p 14) highest manager with responsibility for the day-to-day running of the company, **Chief Executive Officer**

Maori poi dance n (p 68) dance performed by women using balls attached to strings. The poi dance was originally used to increase the flexibility and strength in the women's hands and arms for weaving.

market share n (p 29) the percentage of the market which is taken by a particular product in comparison with competitors' products

marketing n (p 49) the activity of presenting products or services to customers in order to make them want to buy

Marketing Consultant *n* (p 14) someone whom companies employ to give advice about how to market their products or services

mark-up *n* (p 42) amount by which the price of something is increased before it is sold again

meet your brief *v* (p 38) carry out your instructions

milestone *n* (p 55) mark, stage, level of achievement

mission *n* (p 85) company's main purpose

monitor *v* (p 12) watch carefully and record the results

mortgage *n* (p 51) money which you borrow in order to buy a house

N

National Curriculum *n* (U22 T7) the set of subjects that children in England and Wales must study from the age of five to 16

navigation *n* (p 86) moving around and locating of information

network *n* (p 85) linked computers which can share information and programs

networking *v* (p 69) using the opportunity to meet people it might be useful to know

never look back *v* (U9 T16) become more and more successful

niche product *n* (p 33) product which only interests very specialised customers and does not interest the mass market

no end of (U24 T10) a lot of

non-committal *adj* (p 95) not expressing an opinion

nothing to beat (U10 T17) nothing better than

O

occupancy rate *n* (p 72) the average number of rooms occupied in a hotel over a period of time, in this case, a year

off-season *n* (p 67) the time of year when there is less business activity

old hand *n* (U14 T23) very experienced person

on the market *adv* (p 32) for sale

on the road *adv* (U6 T11) travelling to different places

one-stop shopping *n* (p 83) service providing everything you need in one place

online *adj, adv* (p 86) connected to the Internet

online distribution *n* (p 19) the supply of goods through the Internet

online publicity *n* (p 29) advertisements on the Internet

on-the-job training *n* (p 10) training while you are working

opening *n* (U14 T24) job opportunity

opposite number *n* (U24 T11) person who has a similar job to you in a different organisation

opt for *v* (p 33) choose

outcome *n* (p 77) result

outlet *n* (U9 T16) shop

outsell *v* (p 33) sell more than other products

outsource *v* (p 94) employ companies outside the organisation to do part of the organisation's work

outstanding *adj* (p 70) excellent

overheads *pl n* (U5 T8) the regular and necessary costs, such as rent and heating, that are involved in operating a business

P

PA *n* (p 14) short for **Personal Assistant**

packaged *v* (p 32) wrapped and displayed so that people will want to buy

page view *n* (p 83) individual website page read by people logged onto the Internet

partnership *n* (p 52) company owned by two or more people

part-time job *n* (p 17) job which is only done for part of the working week, less than a full-time job

pay a premium *v* (p 31) pay a higher price

payment terms *pl n* (p 43) arrangements made for payment, especially the amount of money and the period of time agreed

PDA *n* (p 82) short for **Personal Digital Assistant**

peak time *n* (p 91) the busiest time

peer *n* (p 13) person at the same level as you in a company

performance *n* (p 14) how well a person or company does

perk *n* (p 18) extra payment or benefit which is not part of your salary, e.g. a company car

permanent contract *n* (p 10) an employment agreement which is not for a limited period of time

Personal Assistant *n* (p 14) someone who is employed to do secretarial and administrative tasks, especially for a manager

Personal Digital Assistant *n* (p 82) mini hand-held computer which has multiple functions such as word-processing, spreadsheet, diary and calendar facilities

personal touch *n* (p 35) having personal contact with and being aware of the needs of every individual customer to make them feel special

phenomenon (*pl* phenomena) *n* (p 94) something unusual or interesting which is extremely successful

pitch *v* (U6 T9) aim, direct

pitfall *n* (U13 T22) likely mistake or problem

plate: a lot on my plate (U23 T9) large amount of important work to deal with

player: big player *n* (U6 T11) large and powerful business

ploy *n* (p 29) tactic or trick, especially when used in marketing

plus *n* (p 65) advantage

point blank *adv* (U10 T19) in a very few words without trying to be polite

point of purchase *n* (p 105) the place where a product is sold

point-of-sales display *n* (p 28) where products are arranged in a shop in a way which advertises them to customers

point out *v* (U23 T9) make clear

pop *v* (*inf*) (p 41) put

post *v* (p 29) pin on the walls

portal *n* (p 86) website which provides information and links to other websites

power cut *n* (U7 T12) interruption in the electricity supply

practice *n* (p 67) method

premium *adj* (U12 T21) higher than usual

place a premium on *v* (p 83) make very important

prepared *adj* (U9 T16) willing, happy

principal *n* (p 52) the amount of money borrowed

PRO *n* (p 14) short for Public Relations Officer, the person responsible for ensuring that the public think well of a company

profit *n* (p 47) money which is earned in trade or business, especially after paying the costs of producing and selling goods and services

profit margin *n* (p 30) the percentage difference between income and sales

profitable *adj* (p 105) bringing advantages

prohibitive *adj* (p 33) so expensive that you cannot afford it

projected *adj* (p 33) planned

promising *adj* (p 12) showing signs of being likely to develop successfully

promote *v* (p 11) give someone a better-paid, more responsible job; (p 29) advertise or publicise a product or service so that people will buy it

promotion *n* (p 19) being given a better-paid, more responsible job

promotional activities *n* (p 28) ways of advertising something

promotional literature *n* (p 78) written adverts and marketing material about a company, designed to encourage people to buy its products or services

prompts *pl n* (p 60) list of key words used to remind you what to say

pros and cons *pl n* (p 97) advantages and disadvantages

provider of choice *n* (p 101) the company people prefer to shop with

public sector *n* (p 69) government organisations

pull together *v* (p 67) create, organise

purchase *n* (p 28) something which you buy

purpose-built *adj* (p 56) designed and built for a particular use

put off *v* (p 76) delay or postpone

put someone on hold *v* (p 25) make someone wait to speak to the person they have called on the phone

put solutions into practice *v* (p 77) act to solve the problem, not just think about it then do nothing

Q

quarter *n* (p 73) period of three months

quit *v* (p 47) give up, leave, stop doing

quote *n* (U22 T8) price someone offers to do a job for / supply goods at

R

R&D *n* (p 14) short for **Research and Development**

rack up *v* (U22 T7) accumulate

rapport *n* (p 107) good understanding of someone and an ability to communicate well with them

real time *n* (p 82) at the same time without having to wait

receptive *adj* (p 19) willing to listen and accept

recognition *n* (U5 T8) appreciation and acceptance

recommended retail price (RRP) *n* (p 42) price at which a manufacturer suggests a product should be sold, although this may be reduced by the retailer

recruit *n* (p 11) someone who has recently started working for a company

recruitment *n* (p 14) the activity of finding and employing new people to work in an organisation

redundancy money *n* (p 46) money paid to workers that a company no longer needs, to compensate for losing their job

referee *n* (p 20) person who gives information about your experience and ability when you apply for a job

refine *v* (U17 T29) improve by making small changes

reflect *v* (p 21) show or represent

register *v* (U22 T7) show, express

reinvent *v* (p 31) change the appearance or characteristics of something, modify

release *n* (p 19) the moment when something is available for the public to buy

relief *n* (U2 T4) person who takes the place of another worker so that he/she can have a break

repeat order *n* (U8 T15) something which you order again

reporting to me (p 16) that I have authority over

repurchase *v* (p 100) continue buying

Research and Development *n* (p 14) the activity of investigating and developing new products

retail *adj* (p 29) selling goods in small amounts to customers in shops; *v* (p 41) sell to customers in shops

retain *v* (p 107) keep

retrospect: in retrospect (p 112) thinking back to something in the past

return on investment *n* (p 100) the profit made from something you nave invested in

revenue *n* (p 100) income from doing business

right away *adv* (U11 T20) immediately

rival *n* (p 65) competitor, company which produces the same products or services as your company

role *n* (p 16) job or function in a company

roughly *adv* (p 83) approximately

round the clock *adv* (U14 T23) all day and all night

routine correspondence *n* (p 14) normal, everyday letters and emails which are not special

rush hour *n* (U19 T3) the busy part of the day when people are travelling to and from work, and towns and cities are crowded

S

sachet *n* (U6 T11) small, closed container made of paper or plastic containing a small amount of something, usually only enough for one occasion

salary *n* (p 10) money paid regularly to employees for doing a job

sample *n* (p 28) small example which shows what the rest of something is like

sample shop *n* (U21 T6) typical representation of what people would normally buy

savings *pl n* (p 53) money which is not spent but is kept to use in the future

scope *n* (p 19) opportunities

screen: get it up on the screen *v* (p 23) see **bring up your details**

search engine *n* (p 86) website which helps you find other websites

sector *n* (p 55) area of the economy

secure a site *v* (p 33) rent a building or part of a building to run a business from

security *n* (p 49) way of making sure that money which has been lent will be paid back

selling point *n* (p 17) characteristic of a product that makes people want to buy it

server *n* (U7 T12) central computer from which other computers obtain information

set up *v* (p 76) organise

set way *n* (p 88) fixed method

shipment *n* (p 111) large amount of goods sent together

sick leave *n* (U19 T3) absence from work through illness or when you say you are ill because you do not want to go to work

sight: at sight *adv* (p 43) payable immediately, when the item is presented

single out *v* (p 65) praise especially

site map *n* (p 88) plan of where to find information on a website and how the pages link together

skill *n* (p 10) ability to do something well, especially gained through training or experience

skip *v* (p 76) not attend a meeting on purpose

slide *n* (p 59) image which is projected onto a screen or wall

slogan *n* (p 29) short, easily remembered phrase used to advertise something

smooth-talking *adj* (p 16) good at persuading people, not to be trusted

snail mail *n* (U3 T5) letters sent by post compared with the speed of email

soar *v* (p 33) rise very fast

social security *n* (p 51) money an employer pays into a government fund to cover unemployment, sickness pay and retirement pensions

sort out *v* (U8 T14) discuss, deal with

source *v* (p 47) find

spectrum: across the spectrum (U18 T1) including the widest possible range of people

spin-out business *n* (p 55) new, separate company based on a original organisation

splash out *v* (U10 T18) spend a lot of money on things you don't need

sponsor *v* (p 35) support financially in order to get publicity for your company

sponsorship *n* (p 28) helping by giving money to an event such as a sporting event and in that way getting publicity

staff development *n* (p 10) expansion of skills and consequent possible promotion for employees

staff retention *n* (p 91) keeping employees and persuading them not to work for another company

staff turnover *n* (p 90) the number of employees leaving their jobs and new ones starting in a company

staffer *n* (p 65) (American English) member of staff

stand *n* (p 34) arrangement of shelves and tables at an exhibition where an organisation offers information, goods or services

stand by *v* (U22 T8) don't change

stand out *v* (p 38) make people notice

start-up *n* (U6 T11) small business that has just been started

state-of-the-art *adj* (p 55) very modern

stem-cell *n* (p 55) cell taken from a person or animal in a very early stage of development that can develop into any other type of cell

stick to *v* (p 40) not change or be forced to change

stir *n* (p 33) a lot of interest

stock *v* (p 42) keep a supply of a product in the shop

straightforward *adj* (p 88) simple and easy to understand

streamline *v* (p 85) make a company, organisation or process more efficient

strings attached (U11 T20) special demands or limitations (on the loan)

study leave *n* (p 13) period of time away from work for study

subscriber *n* (p 65) person who buys a service or a magazine on a regular basis

subscription service *n* (U22 T7) providing a service in return for a regular payment which can be cancelled at any time

supervisor *n* (p 17) person who makes sure people do their jobs properly

supply chain *n* (p 33) the network of companies who bring goods from manufacture through wholesale supply and distribution to a retailer

swallow *v* (U22 T8) accept

switch *v* (p 31) change

T

tailor-made *adj* (p 12) specially designed to meet individual needs

take a seat *v* (formal) (p 41) sit down

take for granted *v* (p 91) believe something to be the truth without thinking about it

take notice of *v* (U23 T9) give attention to

take off *v* (p 33) start selling well, become a popular product

take the plunge *v* (U9 T16) decide to do something risky after thinking about it for a long time

take trouble *v* (p 106) make an effort

takings *pl n* (p 33) income received in a shop from selling goods

target *n* (p 14) goal or objective decided in advance against which performance can be measured

target audience *n* (p 29) person or particular group of people at whom something is directed

target customer *n* (p 106) person or organisation you would like to have as a customer

task *n* (p 31) job

tax return *n* (p 52) information given to the government about how much you have earned in a year

terms: in terms of (p 49) when talking about

terms and conditions *n* (p 41) the details in an agreement or contract

there and then *adv* (U22 T8) immediately

thrive on *v* (U2 T3) really enjoy

tie it into my work *v* (U19 T3) plan it to fit what I have to do

time and time again *adv* (p 101) repeatedly

time: for the time being (U14 T23) for the moment

title effect *n* (p 85) the way the title of a movie is brought onto the screen

top-heavy *adj* (U17 T29) with too many senior managers for the size of the company

track *v* (p 83) monitor movements of, for example, parcels or shipments

track record *n* (p 13) reputation based on things done up to now

trade event *n* (p 38) event within a particular business or industry

trade in *v* (U21 T6) exchange

trade: in the trade (p 89) working in or involved with a particular industry

trademark *n* (p 47) name or symbol put on a product to show that it is made by a particular producer and cannot be legally used by any other producer

treasurer *n* (p 16) the person who looks after the money in an organisation

trolley *n* (U21 T6) cart

turnover *n* (p 33) total income of a company from sales of its products or services; sales

tweak *v* (p 65) change in small ways

24/7 (twenty-four seven) (U17 T29) all the time, 24 hours a day, seven days a week

U

Umukai Polynesian feast *n* (p 68) special meal where traditional food, *kai* (chicken, pork, fish and vegetables), is steamed under banana leaves in a pit of hot stones, an *umu*

understaffed *adj* (U24 T10) without enough employees

up-and-coming *adj* (U14 T25) successful

update *v* (p 25) add new information to

up-front *adj* (U22 T8) honest

upgrade *v* (p 89) improve the quality or usefulness

upmarket *adj* (p 33) expensive, high-quality, appealing to the luxury end of the market

upside *n* (p 85) advantage

uptight *adj* (U19 T3) stressed and easily annoyed

user-friendly *adj* (p 86) easy to operate

user group *n* (p 105) group of people who are interested in your products and can give you feedback

V

vacancy *n* (U4 T7) available job

vendor *n* (p 100) person or organisation who sells something

venture capital *n* (p 52) investment from companies which specialise in high-risk new businesses

vision *n* (U2 T3) plan or hope for the future

voucher *n* (p 185) piece of paper that allows you to pay less for something

W

web browser *n* (p 83) computer program which gives you access to the Internet

website *n* (p 28) computer file with words and pictures which you can reach through the Internet

what really counts *v* (p 65) what is really important

whatever they throw at you *n* (p 107) all their complaints and requests

whet someone's appetite *v* (U18 T2) give someone a small experience to make them more interested

while we're about it (U16 T28) at the same time

wi-fi *adj* (p 64) wireless connection by which computers can connect to the Internet up to a certain distance from where they are usually plugged in

winning combination *n* (p 69) a successful mixture

word of mouth (p 34) people telling each other about how good a product is

words of wisdom *pl n* (U3 T5) very good advice

working party *n* (p 90) small group of people which studies a particular problem or situation and then reports on what it has discovered and gives suggestions

working practice *n* (p 91) way of working

work-life balance *n* (p 90) the amount of time you spend at work compared with your free time

workload *n* (p 12) the amount of work you have to do

workshop *n* (U16 T27) meeting of people to discuss and/or perform practical work

workwise *adv* (U2 T4) as far as work is concerned

would-be *adj* (p 61) wanting or trying to be

wrapper *n* (U10 T18) additional worksheets and other materials

write-up *n* (U6 T11) report, article

written in sand *adj* (U10 T18) not fixed or dependable